D0539534

WALKS

in the Hadrian's Wall area

A guide to thirteen walks
of between three and five miles in length
in and around the Northumberland National Park

Produced and published by
Northumberland County Council
National Park and Countryside Department
Eastburn, South Park, Hexham, Northumberland.

© Northumberland County Council National Park and Countryside Committee 1982
Second edition (revised) 1985

Text by Janet Bleay
Photographs by Karen Melvin
Designed and illustrated by Eric Dale

Old photographs (pages 15, 47, 50, 56, 81) from the Gibson Collection,
reproduced by kind permission of Mr. J. Philip Gibson
Photograph of Lambley Viaduct (page 61) by E. E. Smith
from the collection of N. E. Stead
Photograph of POWs (page 62)
reproduced by kind permission of Mr. J. M. Clark of Featherstone Castle

The maps are to scale of 1: 25000 (2½" to one mile) and are
reproduced from the Ordnance Survey Map with the permission of
the Controller of Her Majesty's Stationery Office
Crown Copyright reserved

Sites formerly in the guardianship of the Department
of the Environment are now cared for by The English Heritage —
The Historic Buildings and Monuments Commission for England.

ISBN 0 907632 02 5

Printed by Unit Offset Limited, Brunswick Industrial Estate, Brunswick Village, Newcastle upon Tyne

Contents

WITH THIRTEEN 1:25000 (2½") MAPS

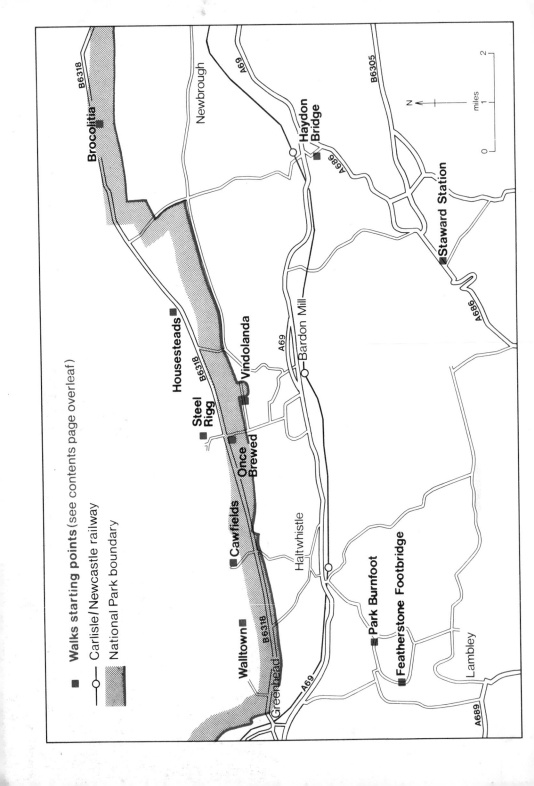

Introduction

THE NORTHUMBERLAND NATIONAL PARK is one of ten National Parks in England and Wales. It is not the largest but within its elongated shape it contains as much, if not more variety of scenery as the larger National Parks.

It is the quality and variety of scenery within the Park that attracts so many walkers and enables visitors to feel a sense both of adventure and of solitude.

The Northumberland National Park Authority is unique in having countryside functions extending outside the Park boundaries. It can therefore help walkers to enjoy following paths outside as well as inside the Park. The combined work of the Authority's staff of National Park Wardens and Footpaths Officers has contributed largely to the walks described in this booklet being readily available.

The aim of this booklet is to provide both visitors and local people with walking routes that they can follow and with interesting information regarding things to see on the way. Whilst it is hoped that walkers will enjoy using the routes described it is also hoped that they will accept the responsibility that goes with using the countryside, and keep the Country Code. This means causing as little disturbance as possible to farm stock, keeping dogs under control, leaving gates as they find them and, of course, not leaving litter to mar the enjoyment of the next walker on the route.

Starting points and transport

There is adequate car parking space at the start of each walk. Sometimes it will be a formal parking area with a hard surface whilst at others it will be a wide enough road verge to accommodate one or two cars at a time.

The four South Tyne walk starting points referred to in this booklet are on, or close to, regular bus routes. The remaining, essentially Hadrian's Wall sites are without a direct public transport service for the greater part of the year. However, during the period from the third week in July to the end of August bus service 890 operates between Hexham and Haltwhistle via the Military Road (B6318) and calls at or near to Housesteads, Once Brewed (Steel Rigg), Vindolanda, Cawfields and Carvoran (Walltown).

National Parks in England and Wales

Some misconceptions surround the term 'National Park' because the Parks are not state owned and neither can they be compared with city parks; they also differ from the wild game National Parks of other countries. The nation may not own them, nor do we have unlimited rights of access over them, but they are certainly nationally recognised as areas of the highest quality scenery in England and Wales.

Northumberland National Park

National Parks in this country came about as a result of Parliament passing the 'National Parks and Access to the Countryside Act' in 1949. The Act did not apply to Scotland which is why we talk only about the National Parks of England and Wales.

Selected as some of the finest remaining remote and open countryside — moor, mountain, valley and seashore — ten National Parks were designated between 1951 and 1957. They exist to safeguard particularly fine landscape and to assist the public to enjoy beautiful countryside for the purpose of open air recreation.

It must be remembered, however, that although an area is designated a National Park, no additional rights of access are automatically bestowed on the visitor. Much of the land in the Northumberland National Park is privately owned, some by the Forestry Commission and some by the Ministry of Defence. So except where the National Park Authority makes special provision, the walker may only go by public rights of way, (i.e. minor roads, footpaths and bridleways) and even then, in the case of Ministry of Defence land, only when it is safe to do so — red flags usually denote areas where it is forbidden and dangerous to enter for the time being.

A National Park Authority has a duty to conserve the landscape of its Park and to promote opportunities for people to enjoy it, but, in the latter case, only when due consideration has been given to the interests of those who live and work in the countryside. After all, it is the past care and attention by generations of landowners and farmers that has been largely responsible for the attractiveness of today's National Park landscape.

A National Park cannot become a rural museum. Farming and forestry practices go on changing, and if the countryside, as the farmers' and foresters' workshop, is to continue to make its valuable contribution to the Country's economy, then the landscape will go on changing and evolving too. However, the National Park Authorities are also planning authorities, and as such have some measure of control over what changes come about in the countryside.

Rights of way and using this booklet

Where hedges, walls and fences mark off land ownership or divide up individual farms, public rights of way make it possible to move across land, which is effectively the farmer's workplace, without interfering with the daily business of making his living.

Apart from public roads (not necessarily 'made up') there are two types of right of way: footpaths and bridleways. Footpaths are simply routes which can be followed on foot whilst bridleways, originally wide enough to accommodate a man leading a horse, may today be walked, or ridden on horseback or on pedal cycle.

As part of the programme involved in the production of this booklet all routes have been examined and signposts, stiles and waymarks provided where necessary. Occasionally a singposted or waymarked change in a section of the path may be encountered. Any alternative route of this kind is planned to cause the minimum of inconvenience to the walker and we ask for your co-operation in following it.

As far as possible maps are drawn with the minimum of fussiness; contour lines for example are omitted to avoid unnecessary visual confusion.

Interpretive notes are printed in the text in normal weight type, but to avoid confusion route directions are given in bold type whilst the letters '(R)' and '(L)' mean 'to the right' and 'to the left' respectively. Also, in the interests of clarity, only those rights of way which form the described routes are shown on the maps, which are all at 1: 25000 (2½" to the mile) scale. The route symbols are as follows:

Footpath ....Bridleway _ _ _ _
Permissive path _ . _ . _ Road _____

The terms 'footpath' and 'bridleway' indicate statutory rights of way and 'permissive path' indicates parts of the routes which walkers are permitted to use by courtesy of the landowner but which have no legal status.

The letters FP and BDWY in the text refer to footpath and bridleway respectively, whilst GR refers to the Ordnance Survey grid reference system, details of which are printed on each of their 1: 50000 series maps.

Enjoy your walk

Comfort is essential to the enjoyment of any walk so wear comfortable sensible shoes or boots where a reading of the route notes might suggest it. Woollen socks, being more absorbent, are usually better to wear than those made from artificial fibres.

Walking may seem to be warm work but, especially at higher levels, it is possible to become chilled. Carry a pullover or jumper which can be put on if the temperature drops, and remember a waterproof will keep out the wind as well as keep off the rain.

A leisurely pace is a comfortable pace. Walks in this booklet have been calculated at roughly 1½ miles per hour to allow enough time for even the least experienced walker to complete the route.

Follow the Country Code

**Enjoy the countryside
and respect its life and work
Guard against all risk of fire
Fasten all gates
Keep your dogs under close control
Keep to public paths across farmland
Use gates and stiles
to cross fences, hedges and walls
Leave livestock, crops and machinery alone
Take your litter home
Help to keep all water clean
Protect wild life, plants and trees
Take special care on country roads
Make no unnecessary noise**

About Hadrian's Wall

Of the first nine walks described in this booklet seven follow the course of the Wall itself for part of the way. This is a well trodden and much written-about area: each walk on the Wall, high on the Whin Sill, in whatever weather, has marvellous views and masses to look at.

Work started on the Wall in AD 122 on the orders of the Emperor Hadrian. Julius Caesar had made brief expeditions to Britain in 55 and 54 BC. Claudius had conquered the southern part of the island in AD 43, but it was not until AD 78, when Julius Agricola became Governor of Britain, that the Romans invaded the north. Penetrating as far as the Moray Firth in Scotland, they built a network of roads with forts and, as part of this cordon the Stanegate was built, linking Corbridge with Carlisle. Vindolanda and Carvoran which feature in three of the walks are Stanegate forts.

Agricola was a wise and statesmanlike general; his son-in-law Tacitus said of him, 'Such was his tact that he made it appear that he had found men loyal, not made them so'. Agricola was recalled to Rome in AD 84 and a calm, albeit tense situation deteriorated rapidly; the Britons were not in favour of being Romanised. After various uprisings and insurgencies the northern Britons rose *en masse* in AD 117 — the first year of Hadrian's reign and not an auspicious start. Accordingly in AD 122 Hadrian himself arrived in Britain and having put many things to rights 'built a wall, 80 miles long . . . to separate the Romans from the Barbarians'. That was, and is, Hadrian's Wall. To avoid confusion, the Wall is now officially called Hadrian's Wall although for centuries it was The Pictish Wall; locally however, it is always known as the Roman Wall.

The fortifications consist of the Wall (all of stone in this section) and fighting ditch to the north; forts, milecastles and turrets along its length to house the garrisons; the Military Way; and the vallum to the south. The milecastles, set a Roman mile apart (1,620yd) measured roughly 50-60ft wide and 57-75ft long internally. Turrets, placed two between

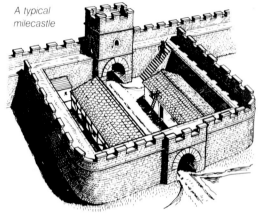

A typical milecastle

each milecastle at a distance of about 540yd from each other, measured about 14ft square internally and 20ft square externally, and were generally watch towers. These two housed the patrolling garrisons. The forts were much larger, housing the fighting garrisons, and contained the Commanding Officer's house, barracks, granaries, hospital, workshops and strongroom. Villages grew up outside most forts, with shops and taverns; the regimental bathhouse was usually outside the fort, too. Housesteads, the biggest and best known fort in this sector of the Wall, and Great Chesters both feature in these walks.

The vallum forms the southernmost limit to the Wall fortifications running more or less parallel with the Wall for its entire length, except at

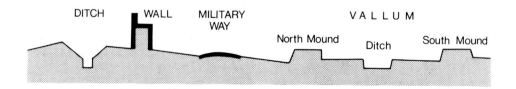

Cross-section of Wall and Vallum

forts where it passes round to the south. Overall the vallum is about 120ft wide consisting of a ditch 20ft wide and 10ft deep with a flat base 8ft wide. The soil dug from the ditch was built into two continuous mounds on each side, set 30ft back from the ditch. They were usually 20ft wide and faced with turf work. There are variations according to what terrain the vallum was traversing; in places the ditch itself is faced with turf on stone flagging, as at Cawfields where the ground is sandy. Over marshy ground it is banked up like a canal; in other places the sides are cut less steeply.

Causeways were built across the vallum opposite milecastles, and at each fort they were controlled by a gateway manned by soldiers from the fort.

The purpose of the vallum was to mark the boundary of the military zone, at the same time providing an actual obstacle to those who weren't supposed to be within the Wall area.

The Military Way was a road built between the Wall and the vallum at a later date than both to replace the piecemeal service tracks that must have existed to get building materials to the Wall. It traversed the length of the Wall, from milecastle to milecastle and fort to fort and probably with a branch off to each turret.

On average it was 20ft wide, had a cambered surface and generally was metalled with small stone and surfaced with fine gravel on a firm base of large stones; it was edged with kerbstones and where the ground was particularly steep the downhill kerbs were particularly large.

For a long time the Military Way was used as a cart track by carriers because its gradient was easier in places than that of the Military Road built in 1751, but now it is completely grass grown and is used principally as a sheep track.

The whole Wall complex is impressive. Place it on the crest of the Whin Sill as the Romans did in this central sector, using all the natural materials to hand, and it becomes one of the most striking features in all England.

The Whin Sill is formed of basalt, which forced itself in a molten state between the layers of limestone, sandstone, shales and coal that cover this area. These were laid down beneath an ancient sea, limestone being produced by lime secreting algae and the calcareous shells of sea creatures. sandstone from river delta deposits and shales from tightly compressed clay. Coal measures were formed when swampy vegetation grew and decayed creating layers of peat which were

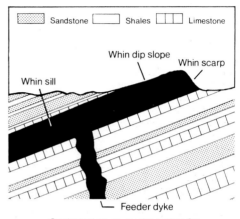

Geological structure of the Whin Sill

then compressed by the weight of sand deposited on top. The molten basalt cooled to form a hard rock, whinstone, in a layer (or 'sill') often over 100ft thick; this stands out today as the steep, craggy north-facing escarpment of the Whin Sill, with gentle dip slopes falling away southwards. During the Ice Age, southward-moving ice scooped out the soft underlying rocks before riding over the hard whinstone, throwing the craggy escarpment into even sharper relief — clearly seen from Steel Rigg car park (Walk 6), or walking back to Housesteads on Walk 7, for example.

The Romans took advantage of this magnificent north-facing escarpment which provided a natural defence and a very hard foundation for their Wall. Whinstone was too hard for them to build with but they were able to quarry sandstone from a number of lesser ridges nearby; Queen's Crags at Sewingshields was one. The stones were generally 6-7in high by 10-11in wide and up to 20in deep tapering towards the back to bond in better with the core. The Romans used the local limestone for mortar; there was a limekiln at Knag Burn, (Walk 7). The whinstone itself was used for infilling along the Wall.

The Romans were here for about 300 years;

Middle Marches showed that the people were as lawless then as they had become by the end of the Roman rule. In the survey the Wall was described as 'an olde mansion or devysion goynge through the said countrey called the peighte wall . . . '. The Commissioners described the condition of neglect and waste that the area had fallen into: '. . . within the said wall endlonge from a place called Wallwyke westwarde unto a place called the wall towne there bene div'se towneshippes and hamlettes that were in tymes past inhabyted nowe lyinge dyssolate and waste.' They itemise in particular Sewingshields Castle and the tower at the Carrowe as being used for summer pasture only although the ground was good for either corn or pasture, and should be worked the whole year. The point was that they were isolated places, too far from any major stronghold to be readily reached if help was needed and so 'true poor men . . . dare not aventure their lyves, bodies and goodes in such uttermoste houses . . . '.

they left the Wall as their memorial. 1,200 years later in 1542, a survey of the East and

𝄢𝄢𝄢𝄢𝄢𝄢𝄢𝄢𝄢𝄢𝄢𝄢𝄢𝄢𝄢𝄢𝄢𝄢𝄢𝄢𝄢𝄢𝄢𝄢𝄢𝄢𝄢𝄢𝄢𝄢𝄢𝄢𝄢

Tynedale

Tynedale had been given the status of a liberty before the Norman Conquest in 1066; and the Normans had never intervened. For 200 years, moreover, Tynedale was in the hands of the Kings of Scotland and its special status continued until the end of the 15th century. For at least 500 years Tynedale had been a place with its own special customs, a place where the King's writ did not run and where any outlaw could flee to escape justice. Even when Tynedale finally came under the King's rule, the inhabitants continued in their old customs which contained a good deal of thieving of cattle, both Scottish and English, rapine and deadly feuds. The whole situation was exacerbated by the Border Wars which had been going on since the late 13th century and in which the English Middle March, which included Redesdale and Tynedale (the two areas which most bothered the authorities) had suffered most. And the 16th century saw perhaps the worst of their sufferings. Between 1535 and 1584 the number of men able to provide Border Service, which they owed by virtue of land ownership, dropped from 93 to a mere 8.

Strongholds, therefore, were a necessity and the castles, bastles and pele towers (all strongholds of varying security) dotted around the country date from this period of border warfare and clan anarchy: Thirlwall (Walks 1 and 2); Blenkinsopp (Walk 2); Walltown (Walk 3); Chipchase and Tecket (Walk 9); are just a few.

The last 300 years or so have seen the steady improvement of land by enclosures of common land, drainage and the application of fertilisers. Lime was the great tonic and this is limestone country. The number of limekilns in the countryside (there is one in nearly every walk) bear witness to the success of the industry which produced quicklime not only for local use but also for much further afield. The farms too, many of them dating from the 18th century and frequently built of Roman stone, illustrate the better times of the past 300 years. Stoutly built, well sheltered, they show as much regard for the terrain as the Romans did building their Wall.

1 Walltown - Thirlwall Castle; return via Low Old Shield

About 3 miles, 2¼ hours. A walk west along line of Wall on Pennine Way to Thirlwall Castle, then north by country roads and upland pastures via Low Old Shield and back to Walltown. History, birds, flowers – and stepping stones over the Tipalt Burn so if the weather is wet and the water high leave this walk to another day – or wear wellingtons.

Park at Walltown car park (GR 675662).

Three walks start from this point. The ancient woods you first pass add a charmed air to a place that is steeped in history (see Walk 3). 'Witches brooms', those twiggy bristles growing in tufts on the branches of the birch trees, are caused by a fungus.

Walk back along the road (west) to road junction opposite Carvoran museum.

The concrete pool to the left of the road close to the junction with the footpath is a water outlet for Walltown Quarry which, although no longer used, still has to have water pumped from it. The Quarry was opened in 1871, employing 40 men at that time and producing about 100 tons a week of whinstone for pavings. It was impossible to quarry whinstone until advances were made in blasting techniques. The Romans never used it because it could not be worked with wedges; they built in sandstone. Once blasted however it can either be reduced to chips for road making or to produce agglomerate.

Paving sets — cobble stones such as you see in market squares, particularly in Scotland — were also produced at Walltown. These were cut by hand from larger pieces of stone after blasting; chisels were used and a laborious job it was too. Whinstone is not generally used for building, but at Walltown the buildings left of the road, one looking like a methodist chapel, were built from large whin stones, all cut by hand.

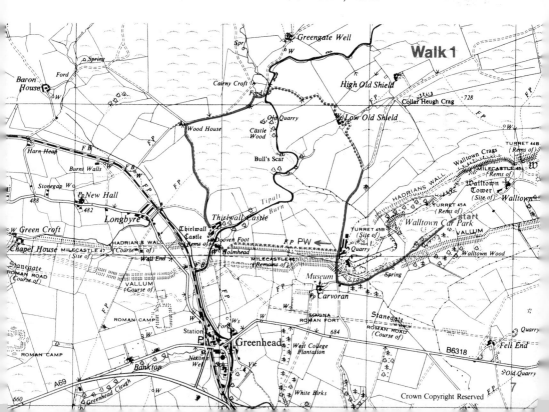

Crown Copyright Reserved

7

At road junction turn right then after about 200 yards cross by stile into field on left to continue along the Pennine Way and line of the Wall and ditch.

With the fighting ditch immediately to the left, filled with rushes, Carvoran is to the south of this. A Roman Army Museum was opened here in 1981 and rather than describe the fort a visit to the site is recommended.

Carvoran is a Stanegate Fort, older than Hadrian's Wall and guards the junction between the Stanegate and the Maiden Way. The Maiden Way was a very long stone-paved Roman road, averaging about 15ft in width, running from Bewcastle in the north via Birdoswald to Carvoran, and thence south to Whitley Castle and Cross Fell to Kirkby Thore in Westmorland. Part of it is now the Pennine Way.

Across this field (heading west) the walk continues with the fighting ditch alongside on the left.

The pink flowers along this stretch include the ragged robin which grows in damp pasture and is one of the first flowers to disappear when fields are 'improved'. Thyme and herb robert occur along the grassy banks and foxglove grows well along the walls. The latter is one of the few plants still used extensively in medicine; the dangerous drug digitalis is extracted from the leaves for the treatment of heart disorders.

The stile at end of field leads over the farm wall.

The stile offers a good vantage point. To the north is Thirlwall Common, then Spadeadam and Kielder Forest. Ahead is Longbyre, a mining village, Greenhead with its golf course at the top of the hill, and the Newcastle to Carlisle railway. This railway was built between 1829 and 1838 but it all started in 1824 when at a meeting of the 'nobility, gentlemen, clergy and freeholders of Northumberland' it was decided to obtain estimates for the construction of a railway and a canal between the two cities. It was reported that a railway would cost £252,488 and the canal £888,000 On the day in 1838 when the whole line was

Train approaching bridge across the Tipalt Burn with Blenkinsopp Hall in the background.
From an engraving after J.W. Carmichael, 1838.

opened the Mayor of Newcastle entertained his opposite number in Carlisle to a civic reception. The Mayor of Carlisle travelled in a train which left Carlisle early in the morning, arriving in good time for lunch. The hapless travellers who set off in the opposite direction from Gateshead to Carlisle, weren't so fortunate. What with mishaps and break-downs, they didn't return for 16 hours or so and since the carriages were open in those days, all 3,500 of them were soaked to the skin.

There had been many objections to building a railway; people refused to believe a steam engine could 'travel at a rate almost equal to the speed of the fleetest horse', and were disgusted at the thought of being conveyed in 'something like a coal wagon'. But the railway was a boon to commerce, especially to the coal owners. The building that looks like the ruins of an ancient castle, north-west of Longbyre, is Baron House, a screening plant for a local coal mine. Here the coal was divided into different grades before being loaded onto trucks and sent down a side track to its junction with the railway. This is just one of many concerns that benefitted from the ease of transit by rail.

From the stile continue downhill along line of fighting ditch, past unexcavated remains of Milecastle 46 until you come to the beech trees. Cross the stile and descend to the Tipalt Burn.

The wall on the opposite side of the ditch is on the line of Hadrian's Wall and is probably built largely of Roman stones. This is a good stretch for seeing the line of the fighting ditch and of the vallum running parallel with it almost as far as the Tipalt. Arrive at the descent to the Tipalt and there are magnificent beech trees which flourish on thin soils and were widely planted in the 18th and 19th centuries.

Thirlwall Castle now comes into view to the north, but first is Holmhead. Now a guest house, it was built on the site of Turret 46A and has a Roman stone, upside down, in one of the outbuildings, recording work done on the Wall by the Dumnonii tribe from Somerset, Devonshire and Cornwall. The local inhabitants provided most of the unskilled labour for building the fortifications.

Thirlwall Castle

Go through gate at Holmhead guest house and cross footbridge over Tipalt Burn. Continue on track past Dooven Foot Cottage.

This point was always one of the weakest along the length of the Wall and it is said that the name 'Thirlwall' was given when the Wall was pierced here by the Scots: they 'thirled' it, or 'threw it down' — hence Thirlwall. The castle was built some time between 1306 and 1346 but no definite date is known, although Edward I is supposed to have slept here on 20 September 1306. In its heyday this castle, built entirely of Roman stones (which explains the lack of Wall between Carvoran and Holmhead) was the stronghold of the de Thirlwalls. Walls 9ft thick, very small windows, and a dungeon kept in good repair rendered it virtually impregnable and it was lived in until the 18th century when Eleanora, the last heiress married into the Swinburn family. They sold Thirlwall to the Earl of Carlisle and it ceased to be inhabited. The east wall fell into the Tipalt Burn in 1831. Thirlwall Castle hasn't a ghost, but it does have a legend . . . The castle at one time fell victim to a marauding band of Scots; a gold table, the pride of the family, was saved from their hands by the skill of an amazingly ugly dwarf who flung the table into the draw well, himself after it, and with supernatural powers drew the top down over him. He is still there, with the table, under the influence of a spell which can be broken only by the only son of a widow — but no-one knows where the well is!

Follow track past the castle, walk past Thirlwall farmyard and take fork (R) uphill.

At the top of the hill you get another view of Baron House (left), and to the right are Walltown Crags and Collar Heugh Crags with High and Low Old Shield. On the far horizon is Burn Divot.

Continue walking north from Thirlwall and bear right along metalled road after passing the cattle grid at Wood House.

Upland pasture this, there's a sheep creep in the wall, right, and a stell, left. To the north (left), the country changes quite dramatically from unimproved land, west, to improved and greener pastures, east. Thirlwall Common was enclosed in 1801, but it still has some of the best mires in the area; Moss Peteral, and further north, Scotchcoultard.

The cattle here are Galloways. Pure Galloways are rare now; they are mostly crossed with a white bull to get a blue-grey colour. They are a slow growing breed but have the advantage of being very hardy and able to lie out where other breeds cannot.

Follow road to Tipalt Burn and cross by the stepping stones.

To the right where the burn bends the force of winter floods has eroded the banks to expose the rock strata and make a marvellous shelter for the sheep.

Several birds have specialised in fast flowing burns, and both the dipper and the grey wagtail nest nearby. The dipper is a particularly interesting species, resembling a large white-breasted wren as it flies low over the water or bobs from boulder to boulder. Most upland birds move downstream for the winter, but their places along the burnside are taken by Arctic migrants like the redwing and fieldfare.

Safely over the burn go through metal gate: follow sunken track and old field boundary, making for Low Old Shield Farm.

The deeply hewn Tipalt Gorge is to the right. Predominantly sandstone, the rock is soft and easily eroded. The gorge is one of the few well wooded areas up here, mainly birch and alder. In prehistoric times birch forests covered all the upland wastes; traces of them can be found where streams have eroded the soil but all of them had disappeared before

Grey wagtail. Adult male has grey upper parts, yellow under parts and black throat

Tipalt Burn stepping stones at Cairny Croft

historic times and the land, nearly all over 600ft above sea level and poorly drained, is mainly used for grazing stock. Rushes grow profusely here; in the winter months they often look as though they have been cut but in fact they have been grazed. If a rush is the only edible material sticking up out of the snow then that is what will be eaten.

At Low Old Shield go through farm yard passing between farm buildings and house. Follow track round front of house and on uphill to join the High Old Shield road. When the road junction is reached turn right.

Low Old Shield must be one of the oldest settlement sites in the area. In the Middle Ages, in upland areas, it was the custom for whole families, with their stock, to move out to the uplands and spend the summer in huts (shielings) where their cattle could be pastured. Few sheep were kept in those days in this area because, before drainage, the damp ground caused foot-rot. In 1599 Camden, on his visit to Hadrian's Wall, saw this custom and wrote of it, 'Here every way round about in the wasts as they tearme them . . . you may see as it were the ancient

Nomades, a martiall kinde of men, who from the moneth of April unto August, lye out scattering and summering (as they tearme it) with their cattell in little cottages here and there which they call Sheales and Shealings'. The custom continued into the 16th and 17th centuries but little remains now of these huts. Often they were built of turf and so disappeared easily. But the word 'shield' is included in a number of place names and this is a typical example. By those standards this is a modern farm, but in fact is at least about 200 years old. Look at the windows on the south face, the sturdy porch built against the wind and the old trees, serving as a shelter-belt to the west.

Follow the track south on metalled road.

It takes you again to higher ground with marvellous views all round. Look back to High Old Shield and, in the distance, the Cheviots. To the right is the Tipalt Gorge, the burn flowing eventually into the South Tyne opposite Bellister Castle.

Continue on road over two cattle grids back to Walltown Quarry, and on past the processing and loading yard. Turn left at buildings and walk back to car.

2 Walltown - Thirlwall - Greenhead; return via Wrytree and Fell End

5 miles, about 4 hours. A walk along the Pennine Way to Greenhead and back to the Wall by lowland pasture and upland bogs.

Park at Walltown car park.
Route description for first part of this walk from Walltown to Thirlwall is described in Walk 1 (pages 7-9).

At the stile just north of Carvoran is a small sign in the form of an acorn; a symbol used throughout England and Wales to waymark long distance paths. This is the Pennine Way. First proposed by Tom Stephenson writing in the 'Daily Herald' in 1935, it stretches for 250 miles along the spine of Britain from Edale in Derbyshire to Kirk Yetholm just over the border into Scotland. From conception to completion it took 30 years: on 24 April 1965 the completion of the Pennine Way was celebrated on Malham Moor. It links 'the high places of solitude' in this country along tracks that have been used from time immemorial and over some of the highest, most magnificent parts of northern England. The Hadrian's Wall area is one of these.

After crossing footbridge at Dooven Foot, turn left at end of cottages and follow track between edge of field and Tipalt Burn. Cross footbridge and turn left over stile to follow FP between railway and burn, all the way into Greenhead.

The Blenkinsopps were the great landowners around Greenhead, probably from before the Norman Conquest, and had their castle on the right bank of the Glenwhelt Valley, just south of the present road to Haltwhistle. Built in 1339 when Thomas de Blenkinsopp had a licence to fortify his dwelling on the borders of Scotland, it was still in good repair in 1416. By 1542 however, the roof had decayed and the family had moved to Bellister. Blenkinsopp Castle is now absolutely in ruins but is very picturesque. The grounds are full of rhododendrons, a species not native to Britain, but brought from the Himalayas in Victorian times. It is so prolific that it is almost impossible to irradicate, and has become a serious nuisance in woods and mountains from the New Forest to Snowdonia.

Station Road developed after the railway was built through Greenhead in the 1830s. The Post Office was once an ale house, the Youth Hostel a Methodist Chapel, and the garage a smithy.

At end of Station Road turn sharp left on road.

This is Glenwhelt, a very ancient settlement with a former coaching inn, The Globe, on the left of the road (the house with the portico), which used to catch the coaching trade on its way down the steep bank from the Military Road. Until 1818 the turnpike road from Haltwhistle joined the Military Road by a very hilly and winding route about a quarter of a mile east of Glenwhelt. When the railway turned out to be a success, however, and coaching became a back number, they found

...re doing poor business at The Globe. ...ally the owners turned from the road at ...front to the fields at the back where ...ming was more profitable.

Glenwhelt had always been a farming community; it was after coal and limestone were found so extensively on the Blenkinsopp lands that the area developed into the prosperous and thriving village of Greenhead. By the end of the 19th century there was a Co-op store, tennis courts, Methodist Chapel, pubs, football and cricket teams, Mechanics' Institute and schools — all based on the prosperity coal had brought. A number of disused pits and quarries around the original Blenkinsopp Castle (Blenkinsopp Hall based on the tower used by the family in 1663 is further down the road) bear witness to this. About 400 men and boys were employed there full-time in 1886 to produce an average output of 2,000 tons a week.

Cross road bridge over the Tipalt Burn and turn immediately right through fieldgate at FP signposted 'College'.

Two stone barns (called 'hemels' up here whether they are small and old or vast and modern) on the left of the path some yards along are all that remains of Glenwhelt Farm.

Follow path through wood behind the vicarage.

Greenhead Church was built in 1827 for £800 and restored in 1880 for over £1,000. Originally a Chapel of Ease under Lambley Parish, the Lambley vicar used to ride over to take services in Greenhead. Now it's the other way round.

Leave wood by stile and follow track over fields to College Farm.

The land at this lower level is noticeably richer than on the uplands around the Wall and the farming pattern differs considerably. Hardy sheep and cattle up on the tops are bred for sale to lowland farmers for fattening. The cattle on this farm are beef breeds with a lot of Charolais in them. Those metal containers are mineral licks for the beasts.

Go through gate to College Farm.

Roman fighting ditch looking west, near Longbyre

17

On the left is a beautifully lined stone drainage channel which goes under the track. Another good piece of stone work is the dry stone wall on the right of the road with the sheep creep in it. The farm was built in the 1880s.

The way now is metalled uphill (L) to Wrytree.

This house was built in 1879 but was a farm long before that. The difference in land and farming between this area and the low-lying College land is already very noticeable.

Follow metalled road around Wrytree Farm to the Wrytree Colliery.

Blenkinsopp Collieries Ltd own this; it is too small to be profitably run by the National Coal Board, but it provides about 600 tons of coal a week to the Stella Power Station near Blaydon. Re-opened in 1965 (because it had certainly been worked in the 1880s and probably even earlier), it is now being worked to a depth of 500ft, taking from the Little Limestone Seam. The tunnel mouth provides both access for the miners and the coal

wagons. The only other evidence of activity in this predominantly rural scene screening plant and the coal lorries.

When Wrytree Colliery was worked in the 19th century it was connected with College Farm, where the oats were grown for the pit ponies and there was a huge chimney for the thresher. The farm was rebuilt after the Blenkinsopp estates were bought by the Joiceys.

After mine gate climb grassy bank to right of pylon, make for plantation and follow wall (R) to minor road via stile. Turn right on road then after 45 yards cross stile (L) and over Painsdale Burn. Follow wall, pass two gates (L) and go through gate at top of field. Turn left, go through gate across track and cross stile to road (B6318). Turn left, cross road and after 150 yards enter field through gate (R). Follow path through farm gate, bear right and walk between large new building (L) and wall. Gate at far end of track leads to Lowtown.

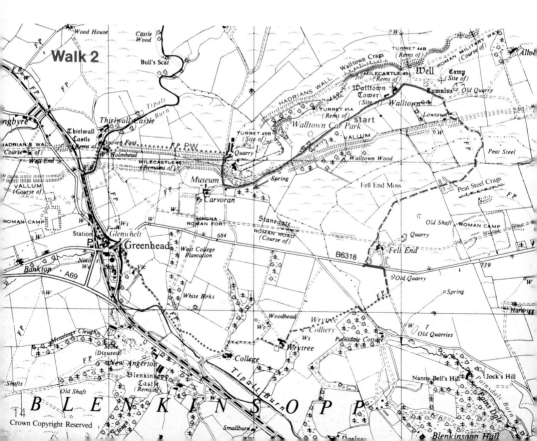

Crown Copyright Reserved

14

Fell End is much older than College Farm, and is built in a position well sheltered by the lie of the land and has extra protection from the belt of sycamore trees. The huge hemel is built right on the line of the Stanegate.

A limekiln, a few yards past the Stanegate, is hardly visible from the path but the track you are on leads from it to an old quarry — convenient for the collection of lime. The coal probably came from the numerous local outcrops. Some old shafts right of the track may have been the source. This is also Haydon Hunt country; they have some easier ground to the south, and in the shire. The Haydon Hunt bounders with the North Tyne Hunt to the north and the Tynedale to the east.

The Whin Sill here flows north and east as if in waves. Peat Steel Crags of the carboniferous limestone group are just to the right. Fell End Moss on the left of this section, once extremely boggy, has been drained and it now supports heathy plants rather than the mossy

types which previously predominated. The shooting butts at the far end bear witness to the success of the scheme. A moss, incidentally, is another word for bog and they are common in this area of the Borders. They give their name to Moss Troopers, those border freebooters who used to infest the area and who, knowing every inch of the way over often treacherous wastes, were able to evade capture after many a raiding party — usually for cattle.

After passing through gates follow waymark arrows around the end of the Moss, cross vallum and follow track to Lowtown Farmhouse.

No longer lived in, this was the shepherd's cottage for Walltown, and just about where the hamlet used to be. The roof, as with many in this area, is stone tiled. The material used for stone slated roofs is always either limestone or sandstone, both of which split easily. The slates at the top are always shorter than those at the bottom since the eaves can stand

Thirlwall Castle in the 1890's

considerably more weight than the ridge. The pitch of the roof is steeper by several degrees towards the ridge as protection against wind and rain. The length of the slates varies from as little as 6in to as much as 36in. Once a roof becomes too dilapidated it is very difficult to replace it with stone slates as they are difficult to get and prohibitively expensive.

Part of an old cheese press stands at the side of the cottage. This part was one of two outsides; a centre piece, cut to fit the grooves, was slowly let down between them pressing the cheese as it went.

Leave Lowtown by gate behind house and follow track to second gate leading onto metalled road. Turn left.

The limekiln slightly to the right with the rock outcrop behind it was a really splendid one, and despite its decay it does show how a limekiln worked. It was in the 16th century that lime, heated and with water added, was recognised as a dressing for sour or acid soil; in the 17th century experts on agriculture constantly recommended its use and by the 18th century farmers were receiving instructions on how to build and operate their own limekilns.

They were usually very simple affairs whereby the farmer made a fire, heaped broken limestone and fuel on it, covered the lot with turf and let it smoulder for a couple of days. The resultant ashes, rich in lime and potash, yielded enough for a season's liming. The kilns so liberally studded about this countryside were probably commercially operated. Kilns were built into the hillside just below rock outcrops to take advantage of the slope of the land: the broken limestone and fuel could be tipped straight in from above. The resultant mixture was raked out from the bottom. Shaped like an inverted cone the kilns were usually built of limestone and sometimes lined with brick.

Today the crevices between the stones provide nest-sites for many birds, and it is not unusual to find four or five wrens' nests in a single kiln. The male wren builds the nests — several dome-shaped ones — each season, using moss, leaves and grass; the female inspects the nests and listens to the male song before she chooses her mate. Having done so, she remakes the nest, lines it with feathers and lays from five to twelve white eggs with small red-brown speckles. During the winter wrens roost communally and an old nest can contain between twenty and thirty birds, huddled together for warmth.

To the left of the road the small trees, protected from stock by wooden frames, have been planted under the National Park Woodland Management Scheme to continue the tradition of hedgerow trees.

Notice the Roman stones surrounding the double stone trough to the right of the road.

Continue on metalled road, past Walltown Farm to return to car park.

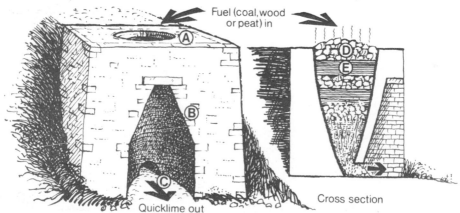

Fuel (coal, wood or peat) in

Cross section

Quicklime out

A. Pot B. Draw arch C. Eye D. Broken limestone E. Fuel

A limekiln was essentially little more than a deep stone bowl reached from the outside by a tall arched entrance chamber. The alternate layers of fuel and fragmented limestone were heated to around 1100°, decomposing and becoming quicklime. This was then drawn out through the kiln eye at intervals of about 24 hours.

3 Walltown - Great Chesters; return via The Loddams and Walltown Farm

5 miles, about 3 hours. A walk eastwards alongside Hadrian's Wall to Great Chesters fort (Aesica), with splendid views from a stretch of Wall that includes some of the Nine Nicks of Thirlwall, and that is not used as much as the Winshields Crags to Sewingshields sector.

The Wall at Walltown Crags looking east

Park at Walltown car park. Go straight up to top of hill and the Wall. Turn right and walk east alongside the Wall.

The first thing you find is the well preserved Turret 45A which looks over Pike Hill, Carvoran and the Haltwhistle Burn. Possibly it was a signal station or forward observation post during the construction of the Wall.

On Walltown Crags are the Nine Nicks of Thirlwall, although two of them have disappeared into the maw of Walltown Quarry. The Nicks, which are a frequent feature along the Whin Sill, were 'joints' in the rock, or points of weakness. It was these points that were deepened by the movement of ice during the last Ice Age to make the depressions you see today.

Wild chives, thin grey-green spiky plants, grow in the crevices below these crags. Camden, headmaster of Westminster School and later Clarenceaux, King of Arms in Elizabeth I's reign wrote that 'the Roman soldiers of the marches did plant heere every where in old time for their use, certaine medicinable hearbs, for to cure wounds: whence is it that some Emperick practitioners of Chirurgy in Scotland, flock hither every yeare in the beginning of summer, to gather such simples and wound herbes; the vertue whereof they highly commend as found by long experience and to be of singular efficacy'. The chive plant is in fact Lilium schoenoprasum and is indigenous to various rocky parts of Britain; so the Romans, while making full use of the plant, probably found it here rather than introduced it.

The route continues along the line of the Wall and behind Walltown Farm.

Walltown in the reign of Edward VI was the seat and lordship of John Ridley, brother of Nicholas Ridley, Bishop of London and Protestant martyr who was burnt at the stake in 1555 alongside Latimer in the reign of Bloody Mary. John Ridley lived in a castellated tower slightly to the north-west of the present farmhouse; the outlines show up beneath the

Remains of Turret 45A looking east towards Walltown Crags

Wild chives

grass. The tower was in ruins by the mid 18th century when one George Marshall Esq built his farmhouse from the stone. George Marshall was 'eminently beloved by his tenants, and the whole neighbourhood, for letting his lands at moderate rents'. The old village of Walltown, which lay south of the farmhouse, has long disappeared.

Climb down the steep slope from Milecastle 45 to Walltown Nick.

At the bottom, in the middle of the gap, is King Arthur's Well (King Arthur is connected by legend with the area) now topped with a man-hole cover. It was said to be here in AD 627 that Paulinus baptised King Egbert (or King Edwin) and several hundred of his followers, but there is little foundation for such supposition.

Cross the stile and continue along the FP (Roman Military Way).

The Roman Military Way was made between the Wall and the vallum to give speedy access between the forts. This is also part of the Pennine Way and the stiles are marked accordingly with the acorn symbol.

Climb up to Muckleback Crag at 860ft.

Milecastle 44 is on the left, and Allolee Farm to the right, sheltered from the prevailing wind by a belt of trees planted to the west. The Wall along this section is nine courses high on its north side but hardly to be seen from the south.

That this is sheep breeding country is evident from the number of sheep creeps right through the line of the Wall. Sheep up here are often Cheviots which, like the Blackface (the other breed used in this area) are very hardy and lamb well in often difficult conditions.

The Military Way is quite clear between Allolee and Great Chesters.

At Cockmount Hill plantation stop shortly after the turret and take a good look at the left hand side gate post on the left of the path. That is a Roman milestone taken from the Military Way.

Cross the stile into the plantation.

The southern end of this plantation is mainly Scots pine but the trees are now old and near the end of their natural span. The northern part of the plantation has been felled and willows have regenerated on the wet ground.

Leave the wood by the stile.

This is a good place to stop for a few minutes and look towards Great Chesters to see the earthworks on the west and weakest side, where four ditches were added to the defences. Cawfields Crags are beyond the fort. In the foreground is Cockmount Hill Farm with its traditional farm buildings and in front of the farm are cultivation terraces, probably medieval rather than Roman.

Walk past Cockmount Hill Farm towards Great Chesters and enter the fort by the west gate.

Great Chesters (Aesica) was built in about AD 128 and, facing east, it guards Caw Gap. This was an infantry fort with the buildings normally associated with Roman forts — gates, towers, a vaulted underground strong room (Roman soldiers required pay), a granary (the Roman army relied far more on corn than meat), administrative offices and shrines. Outside the fort in the field to the east was the bath house supplying hot and cold baths, a steam room, a dry heat room, dressing rooms and latrines.

The water was supplied by an aqueduct, one of the most remarkable construction feats of the whole Wall. It was a channel or 'leat' 4ft deep and wide which started on Saughy Rigg at the head of the Caw Burn, high enough above the camp for the water to feed naturally into the camp. It is 2¼ miles as the crow flies from the source to Great Chesters, but to maintain the height required for this gravity-feed water system the channel took such a winding route that it is 6 miles long. It goes as far west as Benks Bridge (the only place where a bridge was necessary), before coming south to the fort. It is noteworthy that the whole structure was north of the Wall and therefore not protected. Wallis wrote that 'Roman baths were first introduced in Britain by Agricola to give the natives an agreeable picture of a polite, well civilised community'. Possibly the natives weren't impressed and so left the water supply alone. Part of the aqueduct is still visible from the head of Haltwhistle Burn.

Excavation of this fort took place in 1894 when a horde of superb jewelry was discovered in the west tower of the south gate. There was an enamelled brooch in the shape of a hare, a Celtic brooch of gilded bronze generally reckoned to be a masterpiece, a silver collar with pendant, a gold ring and a bronze ring with a Gnostic gem: that is the gem is carved with occult signs. Replicas are in the Museum of Antiquities, The University, Newcastle upon Tyne.

There was a civilian settlement here too, but nothing like as big as the one at Housesteads. The fort, which once housed a 500-strong infantry cohort, provides safe pasture for the now dominant species, sheep.

At the farm turn right and follow the farm track downhill.

There are Roman stones to the right and left of you. At the gate is a truly magnificent gate post at least 6½ft high and with the base deeply buried underground; the whole piece of stone must be colossal.

Turn right again to follow the metalled road and track towards Lowtown. There are three gates so please remember to shut them.

The low mound in the second field on the right is generally thought to be a prehistoric burial mound. The vallum is particularly well preserved all along this sector on your right. Ten crossings, with causeways in the ditch and gaps in both mounds are clearly visible.

The Celtic-Romano "Aesica brooch", gilt-bronze, late second century.

Crown Copyright Reserved

20

Cockmount Hill Farm

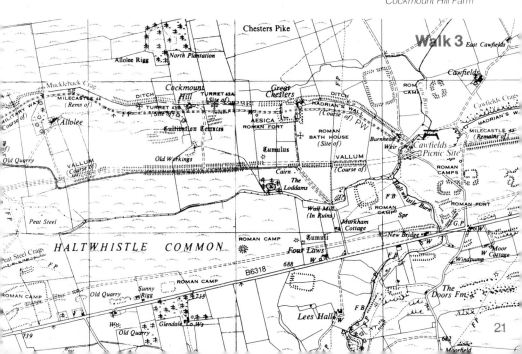

To the left of the track is a small mire known as the Loddams which has developed in the valley bottom where the drainage is poor and the persistent waterlogging has resulted in the gradual deposition and build-up of peat. The ground water is quite alkaline and mineral-rich in this particular site and this has led to the lush growth of a very distinct swampy vegetation of rushes, sedges and tall grasses, together with a variety of willows such as the tea-leaved willow and the bay-leaved willows. The dead Scots pine here probably date from a time when drainage lowered the water level sufficiently for these trees to grow, but with the gradual silting-up of the drainage ditches the water will have risen again and killed the pines. This swamp habitat also encourages a variety of birds such as swallows and swifts which feed on the flying insects, and it is the natural habitat of the sedge warbler — several pairs of which breed in the Loddams.

Further west along the valley the ground water becomes more acid and lacking in nutrients and this has resulted in the development of a quite different type of mire more typical of upland Northumberland. Plants such as cotton grass, heather, cross-leaved heath, sundew and sphagnum moss grow here. The farmer, at some time in the past, has tried to improve the quality of the grazing on the mire by digging a series of open drainage ditches (called sheep grips) in order to lower the water level and encourage the growth of better grasses and herbs which cannot grow in wet mire conditions.

After the fourth gate the track bends right and crosses the vallum. Continue on the track.

After the cattle grid the gate post left of the road is lacking its twin which would have had matching slots, designed for wooden posts to be slotted in and out easily and giving the choice of a one, two or three-barred gate.

To the right is a limekiln with the exposed face of the limestone quarry behind. Close by, the small hill carried a British, that is post-Roman earthwork.

The road now goes past Walltown Farm to the car park.

▨▨▨▨▨▨▨▨▨▨▨▨▨▨▨▨▨▨▨▨▨▨▨▨▨▨▨▨▨▨▨▨▨▨▨▨▨

A variation on this walk is to park at Cawfields Quarry and walk west to Great Chesters. Cawfields Quarry now belongs to the National Park and with the lake and rock face above it is really most attractive; but the mining at Cawfields destroyed a whole section of the Wall right up to Haltwhistle Burn.

Leave the car park at the west end and cross the road bridge.

Where the Military Way crosses the Haltwhistle Burn there was once a Roman water mill, probably used by Great Chesters fort. It was excavated in 1908 when a number of millstones and pieces of pottery were found which dated it to about the 3rd century. The mill house was a rectangular stone building 22ft 9in by 15ft 8in surrounded on three sides by a rampart and ditch. The burn had been widened, deepened and in parts lined with timber. It was one of three water mills built by the Romans along the Wall.

Cross the stile (L) into the field, turn right, pass in front of Burnhead Cottage to Great Chesters via series of stiles. Here enter the fort by the east gate. The route is now the same as already described.

Vaulted underground strong-room at Great Chesters

4 Cawfields - Hallpeat Moss; return via Shield on the Wall

3½ miles, about 2 hours. A walk on upland grazing south of the Military Road, turning north via one of the best-preserved sections of the vallum at Shield on the Wall to climb on to the Wall ridge and back to Cawfields.

Park at Cawfields picnic site.

This site was created in 1974 by the National Park. Until about 1950 the quarry produced whinstone chippings for road surfacing and the rock face, which is so prominent a feature here, is a section through the Great Whin Sill formed 30 million years ago.

Leave the car park at north-east corner and take FP along left edge of quarry lake. Walk through line of Hadrian's Wall by kissing gate with acorn sign denoting Pennine Way. Don't turn immediately right on the wall but gradually bear right to well defined track that goes south across vallum to join metalled road.

Just after the vallum on the right, and a few yards south on the left are the sites of two temporary camps. These, with others in the vicinity, are supposed to have been built for the men building the Wall and perhaps used as training or exercise camps once the Wall was in position.

After joining the road some old limestone workings appear on the left. The stone was quarried both for road building and, more commonly, for land improvement. It was burned in limekilns, the resulting powder then being slaked with water and spread on the land to neutralise the acid soil that predominates around here.

Walk up to crossroads (Military Road B6318) at Milecastle Inn. Cross straight

This section through the Whin Sill, left exposed by quarrying, can be seen at Cawfields

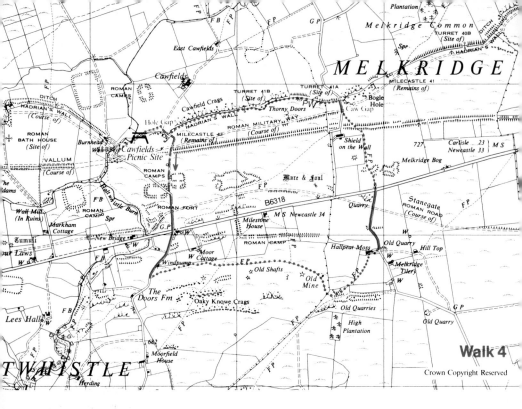

Crown Copyright Reserved

Walk 4

over (beware fast traffic) and continue on up road in direction of Haltwhistle.

This used to be called the Common Inn, possibly because it was on Melkridge Common. Another name for it, used locally, was the North Jerry. The 'Sportsmans Inn' at Coanwood was known as the 'Coanwood Jerry' or 'South Jerry'. The word 'Jerry' was short for 'Jerry-Shop' which in the 19th century was a low dram shop, in other words, a public house.

Proceed on road uphill.

Tree cover here is sparse so the hawthorns, the remains of the field hedge, are a welcome sight. There are also bilberries on the road side which fruit between July and September. To the right (west) are good views over Haltwhistle Burn winding south to the Tyne, with the difference between its improved farmland and the more bleak upland landscape to the north being very marked.

100 yards after passing house (L) climb ladder stile into field (L) to FP signposted

'Hallpeat Moss.'

Walk behind the limekiln; it is derelict and unsafe so don't explore. The lime came from the quarry on the right near Oaky Knowe Crags.

The soil here is peaty and Hallpeat Moss gets its name from being a place where peat was cut for the Hall, in this case probably Willimoteswick. Most of the Melkridge land belonged to the Ridleys of Willimoteswick and in 1772 Hallpeat Moss Farm was owned by John Ridley, known as 'The Chief Ridley'.

Keeping dry stone wall left continue towards farm, following main track.

The lumpiness of the ground can probably be attributed to past coal mining activity. The views to the left on a fine day show the Wall cresting the Whin Sill with Winshields Crags prominent at 1,128ft, and Hopealone GPO repeater tower showing among the trees of Wark Forest. Hopealone was one of the lonely outbye farms until, with many others, it was swallowed by the forestry planting before the second world war.

The path on the ground here is indistinct but bear south-east towards crags and limekilns.

The small pond is fenced-off to prevent animals becoming bogged down. The ground here is also usually pretty wet so take care when walking through the rushes.

Go through the wicket gate ahead towards well preserved limekilns. Bear left just after these and cross wall by stone stile into field. Cut the corner of this field to stile alongside gate. From here head diagonally uphill on line to farmhouse. This field is used as a hayfield so please respect the farmer's livelihood by walking in single file.

Hallpeat Moss Farm is in the true tradition of Northumbrian stonebuilt farmhouses with the farm buildings on each side. The stone flagged roof, becoming an increasingly rare sight, is still intact. Notice the flags starting narrow at the top of the roof and widening at the bottom. This is a precaution against both rain and gales.

At the farm turn right and follow edge of field to leave it via stiles and onto road.

The beech trees along the side of the road are fast disappearing. They used to be a magnificent sight but have had to be felled one by one due to decay. The National Park have now carried out a replanting scheme with the as yet small saplings securely fenced off from farm animals until they are big enough to withstand grazing.

At road turn left and go up to Military Road. Cross to stone stile and climb over to farm track leading past Shield on the Wall. Keep fence and wall line left.

A couple of fields to the left of this track are two tall stones (there used to be three about 200 years ago). They are thought to be the remains of a Bronze Age circle. They are called the 'Mare and Foal', and are very useful for animals to rub themselves against. An amazing number of Roman altar stones and

pillars and other large pieces of stone were set in place by farmers in the past to provide their stock with rubbing stones.

Shield on the Wall Farm is ahead, left. The name 'shield' is a sure indication that this was one of the summer grazing grounds where a family came for summer pasture for their stock, and lived themselves in the shielings or huts.

At the end of the stone wall follow waymarking and cross vallum diagonally.

The stretch of vallum between here and Haltwhistle Burn is about the most perfect throughout the whole length of the Wall. It is not just a ditch dug out to mark the military zone; it was strongly built, the sides being revetted in turf-work, capped with clay and founded on flagging. There are various gaps for crossings, although these are not set at regular intervals. Three of them are just west of the farm.

After the vallum walk round the end of the ridge and cross ladder stile to the road. This is Caw Gap. Turn right, walk up road 45 yards and at sign 'Milecastle 42' go through wicket gate (L) and bear right to the line of the Wall and Pennine Way.

Far to the north-east (right), are the Simonside Hills and more directly north Wark Forest, this part planted in 1938. Take a bearing from Hopealone Mast, move west by south and that solitary speck on the horizon is Burn Divot, a haunt of outlaws and cattle thieves.

Limekilns near Hallpeat Moss

Many an honest drover is supposed to have met his end there, his body easily dumped in the surrounding wastes. It is said that lights, flickering around the windows at night, are the ghosts of those murdered in the house. The date 1737 is carved on the lintel. Ideally situated to watch out for excise men, this now desolate building once housed an illicit still — and that is what it is chiefly remembered for.

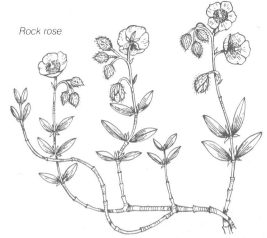

Rock rose

Closer in to the Wall the land is much improved due to the exertions of the farmers over the past 200 years. Before that, and particularly as far as the land now under forestry cultivation was concerned, methods were not sufficiently advanced to provide enough crop for all-year-round grazing, so these lands were used for summer pastures. After the advances in agricultural methods in the 18th century and the enclosure of lands which meant that farms could be better managed, the area became more permanently inhabited and for a while there were enough children locally for there to be a school house at Bridge End, a mile north of Caw Gap. With the drop in the rural population this school and others like it closed. Cawfields Farm, 540 acres, is an excellent example of a farm that has survived.

It is unusual to see acid-loving plants like the foxglove growing alongside lime-loving plants like the rock rose, but whilst the sandstone is strongly acidic, the whinstone (basalt) is alkaline. This means that although there is no limestone here, plants that need a 'basic' soil can survive. Straight ahead are the Nine Nicks of Thirlwall and below, left, a prominent section of the vallum.

Follow the line of Hadrian's Wall — and come to Milecastle 42.

Excavated by John Clayton in 1848, 63ft by 49ft internally, the walls are 7 or 8 courses high and 8ft thick. The masonry at the gateways is massive and in the south gate you can see a bar hole for the doors. Apparently the milecastle was built at two distinct times. Three milestones were found just south of here on the Military Way. There was a great upsurge of interest in the Roman Wall in the last century especially when knowledge of it was increased by observations based on scientific excavations of sites. John Clayton was one of the archaeological 'giants' of the Wall. Another was Collingwood Bruce

who, a year after the excavation of Milecastle 42 led a party of 'Pilgrims' along the Wall, henceforward for many years to be an annual event, and they christened the next gap 'Pilgrims Gap', although it is normally called Hole Gap. That is a natural phenomenon, unlike Cawfields Quarry, to which you are now returning through the wicket gate. If the Romans had possessed the know-how to blast the whinstone into chippings to make roads (the practice that later created Cawfields Quarry) they would have had a much easier time than cutting, carting and laying all those millions of paving stones to line the stanegates and other military roads!

Return to car park via the wicket gate.

5 Once Brewed - Melkridge Tilery; return via Shield on the Wall and Peel Cottage

4½ miles, about 3 hours. Starting from the Once Brewed Information Centre the walk takes you south of the Wall, over the Stanegate and through fields to Melkridge Tilery, thence north, over the Military Road up to the Wall and along the highest stretch along Winshields Crags with marvellous views on a clear day.

Park in Information Centre car park: go out onto B6318 (Military Road) and walk past Twice Brewed Inn on left.

First on the left is the Once Brewed Youth Hostel, then the Twice Brewed Inn. When Lady Trevelyan opened the Youth Hostel in 1934 she said that she named it the 'Once Brewed' because, while it was well known that ale had to be brewed twice, it was to be hoped that the tea at the hostel would only be brewed once!

The cottage beyond the Twice Brewed is West Twice Brewed Farm and this, too, was once an inn — it is much larger inside than it looks, having cellar, its own well, and a huge bedroom upstairs which provided space for dancing. The biggest inn, however, was further back down the road at the East Twice Brewed, now a farm. As many as 20 men and 50 horses stayed here overnight. It was here that Hutton, making a 'Wall' pilgrimage on foot at the age of 78, having succeeded only with great difficulty in getting a bed to himself for the night, sat amazed at dinner as he watched the carriers eat. He saw them consume boiled beef, equal to about half a beast, followed by a pudding equal to a peck measure, and each man put as much down his throat at one swallow as lasts most men for a whole meal.

After about ¼ mile leave the road by a stile on the left set back next to black shed opposite The Vallum guest house. The FP leads alongside farm wall to Brackies Burn. After the burn turn south-west aiming for the ruins of North Seatsides, cross two wooden stiles and head for the deserted barn on the hill top.

North Seatsides used to be the shepherd's house for Seatsides Farm, itself built on the site of a Stanegate fort. The next fields are hayfields so walk in single file. The turf here is very old and supports a remarkable variety of flowering plants. In general, the greater the variety of plants, the older the meadow. There

are certain plants such as the yellow or hay rattle, (so called because if you shake it when the seed capsule is dry, the seeds inside shake about and make a rattling sound), used as indicators by ecologists to assess the quality of meadowland. Top quality from the naturalist's viewpoint is not assessed in harsh economic terms, so old meadows are becoming scarce and therefore more valuable.

Yellow rattle

Cross the stone stile by the barn and walk south-west. The track is not very clear but follow the waymarking signs for about 300 yards to a stretch of derelict stone wall and then again head south-west downhill for the far corner of the field where there is a stone stile to cross onto the farm road.

The northern boundary of this field follows the line of the Stanegate and there must be a good few Roman stones in its construction. The soil up here is acid and wet which is why there are so many rushes: the sheep use them for shelter and the cattle use the stony outcrop by the wall where the stile leads to the farm track.

Cross stone stile. Turn right and follow track to gate at end.

This is a continuation of the road linking the routes between Henshaw — Military Road and Melkridge — Military Road, two of the ancient townships of the area. To the left is Bayldon Farm; to the right is a particularly good stone wall, thick and strong with its throughs, pronounced 'thruffs', to give it extra support. Shelter for stock is essential up here and a really good, high stone wall is the best; it keeps the livestock in and the winds out. A thick hedge is probably a close second. A sure sign of stormy weather is when the beasts or sheep gather up close to the farm buildings or shelter in the lee of the walls.

At the end of the track climb stile onto road. Turn right, go through first gate (R) into field and head for the ruin on the hill top.

This is, indeed, called 'Hill Top' and provides marvellous views to the south over the South Tyne Valley and Plenmeller Common. Not surprisingly since it is so exposed, the roof of this building blew off during a storm in the late 1970s, taking with it most of the supporting rafters.

Pass in front of the house, climb stone stile into next field and cross to the wooden stile leading to road.

Melkridge Tilery on the left was built about 200 years ago: tiles and pipes were manufactured there. Coal outcrops here as well as clay, and in the 19th century the tilery was combined with a small coal mine, the two providing work for 23 people, full time, in the 1880s. The coal,

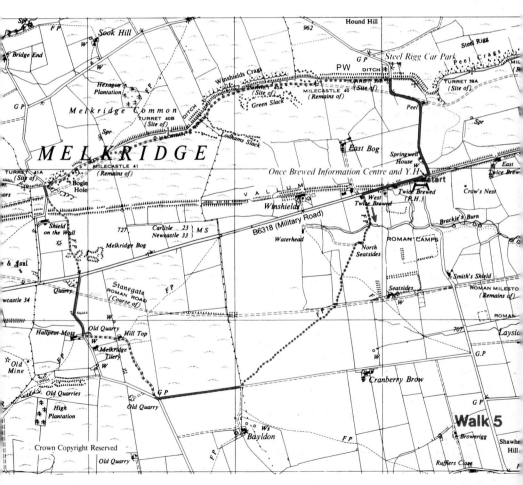

View north from Hill Top

won at about 120ft down, was sold locally.

After stile turn right and follow road to junction with Military Road. Cross carefully to stone stile opposite and go over to farm track. Shield on the Wall farm is ahead, (L).

The vallum behind the farm is one of the best preserved stretches along the whole of the Wall and is described in Walk 4 (page 25).

Cross the vallum, walk round the end of the ridge over the stile to the road. Turn right, cross stone stile (R) and go up steep slope alongside the Wall and Pennine Way which you follow for some 1½ miles.

With Melkridge Common lying to the north of the Wall, Milecastle 41 (Melkridge) is at the beginning of the first gentle ascent and Turret

40A is at the top. The soil here is peaty, acid and shallow, supporting heather as the main type of vegetation. Lodhams Slack at the beginning of the crags and Green Slack near the summit are shallow depressions, 400-500yd long, produced by natural erosion of the Whin Sill; both have been made use of for defensive purposes, not by the Romans, but by native British inhabitants; there is an earthwork at the base of Lodhams Slack and a number of hut-circles in the shelter of Green Slack.

After Turret 40A you come to the summit of Winshields Crags where the panorama is tremendous. From a height of 1,128ft you can see to Criffel in Kirkcudbrightshire westwards, wave upon wave of Whin Sill and Wall to the east, southwards look over the Tyne Valley to the Pennines, and westwards the Nine Nicks of Thirlwall and thence as far as the Solway. Then there are the farms, each with its shelter belt and inbye land. 'Inbye' is a term used in northern England and in Scotland for the small enclosed fields near a farmhouse which formerly received all the manure from the farm's livestock, making them suitable for constant cultivation. Fields 'outbye' by contrast, rarely received any dressing and were used mainly for grazing. By extension the two terms have come to mean places close to the centre of the parish, and places far out at the parish boundary.

These heights give a tremendous feel of impregnability. Someone must have felt this in Elizabeth I's reign because he wrote to the Queen suggesting that the Picts' Wall be

View east from Winshields Crags

made the frontier between England and Scotland. Like Hadrian, he reckoned that this was a narrow, well defined line that could easily be held by only a few men. He put forward his suggestion in 1587, the year when Mary Queen of Scots was beheaded and the English Middle March suffered some of its bloodiest raids. The proposal was for the Wall to be reconditioned and skonses set up, each a mile apart, something on the lines of the milecastles, and for these to be manned by ten gunners apiece. Only these men would be paid, their commanders being recompensed by the grant of 1,000 acres each at 1d per acre in the vicinity of his particular skonse. The author estimated that Hadrian had spent £19,000 on building the Wall; the cost to Elizabeth, he said, for reconditioning would be a mere £30,000 — which allowing for the rate of inflation since AD 122 wasn't bad and likely to appeal to a Queen who was notoriously tight-fisted. Apparently, however, it did not because nothing further was heard of the scheme.

The concrete block is a trig point marker, used by the Ordnance Survey in map making. The telescope was erected by the owner of Winshields Farm whose predecessors, the Armstrongs, farmed it for 400 years.

From Winshields continue eastwards alongside the Wall to the road.

While heather grew fairly profusely further back on the shallower soil, bracken has replaced it here where the soil is deeper. This plant is poisonous to cattle at certain times of the year, and although it is widely eaten in Japan where the tips are regarded as a delicacy, it is known to be carcenogenic. There is evidence that it is spreading in many upland parts of Britain, but it is very expensive to control. It is, in fact, one of the oldest plants; in fossil form brackens date back more than 300 million years.

After Milecastle 40 the Wall, hitting a patch of sandstone, disappears, although the ditch to the north of it is well preserved. Where the Wall was vulnerable on low ground or in a hollow, the ditch was made particularly strong; so there is no ditch, for example, below Winshields Crag, but a strong one where the Wall weakens, as here, and in the gap at the road.

At the road turn right and walk down past Peel Cottage and thence over the Military Road to the Once Brewed car park.

A pele tower was said to have stood just behind the present Peel Cottage, on the line of the Wall. This would account for its name, but there is now no trace of any such building.

Approaching Steel Rigg from the west

6 Steel Rigg - Hotbank; return via Peel Crags

4 miles, about 2¼ hours. This walk takes you north of the Wall to Hotbank Farm and then back along the line of the Wall to Steel Rigg. This way the Wall is seen from both sides: the crags towering above you on the way out – the view the 'barbarians' had, and on the way back what the Romans saw – countryside for miles around. Furthest point of the walk is Hotbank Farm with Crag Lough shimmering in the foreground.

Park at Steel Rigg car park.

The walk starts from this car park, itself built on the line of the Wall. Situated about a half mile to the north of Once Brewed Information Centre, Steel Rigg is within easy reach by those on foot. See notes under ' Starting points and transport ' on page 1.

View north-west from near Steel Rigg

Leave car park by main entrance: turn right along road for 200 yards to gateway and finger-post sign 'Hotbank 1½ miles' (R). Cross stile and walk along farm track.

To the right of the track shortly after the gate, the dips in the ground mark an old quarry. This is limestone country: Steel Rigg ridge, the low mound in the foreground to the right, is limestone, through which the molten magma forced its way to form the Whin Sill.

Peatrigg Plantation on the left is mainly Scots pine and birch, a tree association characteristic of dry uplands and the ancient Caledonian Forest. Look across from here to Peel Crags, which are popular with rock climbers. To the left (east) of the crags are Cat Stairs, a great gash in the Sill, filled with enormous boulders tumbled down from the Wall.

Hotbank Farm

Continue on track past Peatrigg barn and on to Long Side barn.

Peatrigg is a Dutch barn, combined with an older stone hemel, now used for hay. Distant left is Hopealone GPO Mast and Wark Forest. Planting started in 1938, 1,000 acres annually. Eastwards wave upon wave of hills follow the pattern of the Whin Sill.

After Long Side barn, again used for hay, continue to the farm wall, waymarked, and cross stile with sheep fold (L). Go straight ahead for a few yards to the ditch (sike) which divides the parishes of Melkridge and Thorngrafton. Bear right at sike, then left over the sike at waymark. These are hayfields so please walk in single file heading for the left hand edge of Hotbank Crags. After the second stile, go through the gate and follow cart track (R) to Hotbank Farm. The next gate leads into the farmyard. Cross farmyard and go over stone stile

beside gate. Turn right and follow the line of the Wall, heading west.

At this point you have rejoined the Pennine Way. Hotbank Farm has been owned by the National Trust since 1942.

Milecastle 38 is visible on the ground here and a National Trust panel gives information about it. The track then runs down to Milking Gap. When the Wall was planned a fighting ditch on the north side of the Wall was envisaged as an integral part of the whole scheme. Shortly after building commenced, however, plans were changed and the ditch declared obsolete. But wherever a gap appears in the natural defences, as at Milking Gap, the ditch reappears as a precautionary measure. Here it runs just to the right of the path and continues into the wood at Crag Lough until it reaches High Shield Crags. Also at Milking Gap, as at the other gaps, the Wall

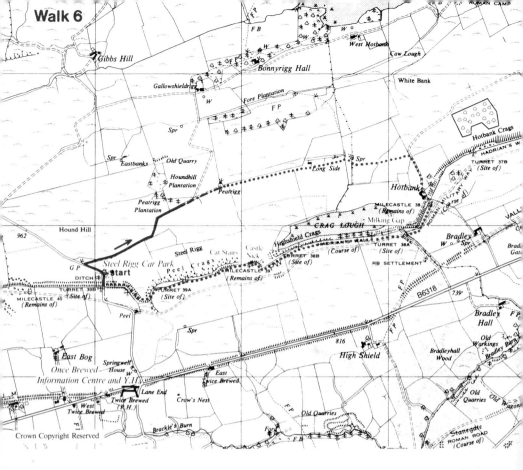

Crown Copyright Reserved

has been built so that it turns into the gap and then out again at the other side. This enabled the Roman soldiers to enfilade any attackers who had breached the ditch and to pick them off from two sides instead of straight on from one side only.

Cross ladder stile to farm track, then right over stile alongside cattle grid to north side of Wall. Walk west over another ladder stile, into wood and up to top of crags above the lough.

It was near to Crag Lough that Hutton, writing in 1801, noted a 60yd stretch of Wall still standing 8ft high. William Hutton was an extraordinary man. In 1801, at the age of 78, he walked the whole length of the Wall, having first walked from Birmingham to the Lake District. He walked the Wall in both directions and then walked all the way back to Birmingham — a distance of 600 miles.

Throughout he wore a black suit, carried a bag and umbrella and an inkhorn. One pair of shoes lasted him the whole journey and he scarcely wore a hole in his socks. He was accompanied by his daughter Catherine and the routine was that he rose at four in the morning and walked to the next stage; Catherine rose at seven and, following by horse, joined him for breakfast. He then rested for 2 hours before setting off again while she went on ahead to bespeak dinner and lodgings for the night. At times the weather was so appallingly hot that he had to undo the buttons of his waistcoat!

Crag Lough Wood itself is Scots pine and sycamore. Higher up bracken grows, and right on the rop rowans and hazels find a very precarious footing on the crags themselves. The National Trust have done quite a lot of maintenance work in this wood, putting in

35

steps and rails to ease the problem of path erosion.

Crag Lough is a shallow lake that has developed in a depression that was formed by glacial erosion during the last Ice Age. In the 17,000 years or so since the retreat of the glaciers the lough has gradually grown smaller as a result of a continual deposition of organic matter by the loughside vegetation which slowly accumulates and eventually rises up above the water level. This process is called 'succession' and you can see various stages of its progression at different points around the lough: from the initial colonisation of shallow open water by various water plants, through the swamp stage (at the west end) where there is a thick mat of vegetation at about water level, to the stage where the accumulation of organic matter rises sufficiently above water level for willows and other shrubs to grow successfully (as at the east end). The swamp at the west end of Crag Lough is particularly interesting botanically since it is fed by quite alkaline water from the adjacent limestone ridge and this has resulted in the development of a great diversity of different plant species. There are various water fowl here too: mallards, tufted duck, coots which nest in the reeds at the sides, and swans which often nest here too.

Tufted duck and drake

The fishing on Crag Lough is private. Up to 20 years ago there were only coarse fish, mostly pike. Now it is restocked every year with trout to provide game for the fishing club who have the water.

Take care walking along the crags above the lough.

The drop here is considerable, but the view is superb; Barcombe Hill rears up to the south, where stone was quarried for the Wall. Further south Langley Chimney, 100ft tall, looms up on the moors; it used to carry away the fumes produced by lead smelting. At your feet are the tops of basalt rocks — huge columns split in places from the main body of rock, towering above the lake.

On the descent to the next gap the Wall is 'stepped' to keep the courses horizontal while descending steeply. Castle Nick is in the next gap. This milecastle is in excellent shape with its two gateways and officers' quarters clearly visible. As Castle Nick is fairly inaccessible from the south the stones used to build it are small and easily manhandled. No wagon would be able to get up to this point.

It was first excavated in 1854 by Clayton, one in a long line of distinguished historians of the

Wall. At one time Town Clerk of Newcastle, he lived at Chesters and carried out the first scientific excavations of forts and milecastles. His pride in the Wall was such that whatever portions of it came on to the market he bought, to save them from probable destruction. He also restored several sections of the Wall.

Continue on well defined FP alongside Hadrian's Wall.

At Cat Stairs, a steep tumble of stones that you saw from the north side of the walk, there is a way down to the north of the Wall where, by standing below Peel Crags and looking up at the huge pillars of basalt that form the cliff, you get a very impressive feeling of its scale. This is not, however, a right of way.

The fine length of Wall on Peel Crags owes its survivial to F.G. Simpson who excavated it between 1909-11. On the north side chamfered stones were found, apparently coping stones from the top part of the Wall; this is one of the few pieces of evidence to suggest that the Wall was topped by a rampart walk.

Follow the FP down very steep west end of Peel Crags: use the steps. From the base, with the ditch again visible to the north and where the ground in Roman times was probably a swamp, follow the path back to the car park.

The National Trust have restored this section and ask that the public walk beside rather than on the Wall to prevent further erosion.

Peel Crags looking east from Hadrian's Wall

7 Housesteads - King's Wicket - Hotbank; return via Cuddy's Crags

4 miles, about 2½ hours. From the top of the Wall ridge this walk gives marvellous views all round and four of the Northumbrian Loughs can be seen - Crag, Greenlee, Broomlee and Grindon. From the lower ground north of the Wall you get the Picts' eye view of what they had to tackle if they were feeling warlike.

Park at Housesteads car park.

Housesteads was for a long time the seat of the Armstrongs, a most terrible family of thieves and cut throats, just about the worst of the Border clans. They sold Housesteads in the 17th century for about £50 and emigrated to America, which was probably a good thing. About 200 years later John Clayton of Chesters bought it and his family conveyed it to the National Trust in 1974; the fort itself is in the guardianship of The English Heritage. Information about it is obtainable from the information panels at the car park, the museum adjoining the fort and at the Information Barn, jointly run by the National Trust and the National Park Authority.

Hadrian's Wall bridging a burn east of Housesteads

Leave car park by gate at north-west corner past Information Barn and follow track to Housesteads Fort. If you wish to look around fort and museum then you will need to pay an admission charge at the museum. If not then skirt around south side of the fort and east alongside Wall to the Knag Burn.

One reminder of the non Roman past of Housesteads is a bastle-house, built onto the south wall of the south gateway to the fort; making full use of the fine workmanship of the Roman masons. The Armstrongs inhabited Housesteads in the 1500s (infested might be a better word for such a clan) and were probably responsible for building this snug little stronghold against the Roman masonry and, by breaking through into the guardchamber, fitting up a drying kiln for corn.

From fort go right and downhill to the Knag Burn.

This is Knag Burn Gate where the Wall has been built across the burn which eventually flows into Grindon Lough. The remains of two guard houses stand on each side of a gate built into the Wall in the 4th century. The only other gate like this, apart from those at forts

and milecastles, is at Portgate north of Corbridge. Knag Burn Gate was possibly a trade route for the passage of goods north and south and room was provided for the examination of goods and payment of tolls. The bath house for Housesteads fort stood on the east bank of the Knag Burn opposite the middle of the fort. It was heated and the water supply presumably was the fenced spring, encased in Roman masonry, nearer the Wall. The remains of the bath house went, at some time, to build the stone walls nearby. Opposite the spring but on the west side of the burn the remains of a Roman limekiln were found; the Romans used lime in the preparation of their mortar.

There are a lot of nettles around here, especially north of the gate; the Romans introduced one type which they used as a cure for rheumatism. They also used it as a rub to stimulate the blood flow — they must have been warned about the weather before they came!

Cross the Knag Burn by the stone bridge. Head uphill keeping Wall to your left to stile at north-east corner of field. Cross into Housesteads plantation.

This is mostly Scots pine and sycamore.

The Wall, looking east from Housesteads

Leave wood by stile at east end and follow track east.

The stone walling on the left of the track, on the line of Hadrian's Wall, has recently been renewed. The National Park Authority has an Upland Management Scheme, whereby stone walling, which is a traditional craft in these parts, is carried out on behalf of and in co-operation with upland farmers. This part of the Wall at Turret 36A, a signalling post, is called Kennel Crags and at the end of the Crags is Milecastle 36. The turf on these heights is covered with thyme and, depending on what time of year you come, ladies finger, hawkweed and bedstraw.

Walk east over Clew Hill and King's Hill still following the Wall.

At the base of King's Hill is Busy Gap, a wide break in the basalt ridge used with great frequency by the Moss Troopers in the days of border warfare. In Newcastle they actually had a term for it: a 'Busy Gap Rogue' was the utmost in terms of opprobrium. Camden, Court Historian to Elizabeth I, had been too frightened to go anywhere near the place. Two watchmen were ordered to stand here from sunset to sunrise, on pain of forfeiting 6s 8d, to give warning of thieves or of a fray. A

network of these watches was set up from Thirlwall to Walwick, at major river crossings and in the townships.

Where the ground drops down after King's Hill cross stile (King's Wicket); from here the FP heads back westwards slowly traversing hollow to a new plantation on ridge. The path on the ground is indistinct so this may be a good place to sit and peruse the map page.

The gate beside the stile closes the gap made in the Wall for the drove road from the north. At King's Hill there are signs of a Celtic earthwork, the Black Dyke. Running from Tarset in North Tyne it comes south, via the Wall at King's Hill to a point on the South Tyne below Bardon Mill. It was, like Offa's Dyke in Mercia, a boundary probably between Anglian settlers in the east and the Celtic kingdom of Rheged of Strathclyde in the west. Formed of earth upcast to the east side of the ditch (that is, with the ditch facing west) it wasn't a continuous line; rather it strengthened the gaps between various bogs and crags.

Walk west along ridge parallel to the Wall, following waymarking to the new plantation.

Looking back from the ridge, King's and

Queen's Crags are visible. Here tradition has it that King Arthur and Queen Guinevere were sitting one day, one on each crag. The Queen was engaged in arranging her hair when she said something to vex her lord. Indulging in a bit of horseplay he picked up a rock nearby and threw it at her — a distance of only about ¼ mile. Guinevere neatly fielded the stone on her comb to make it fall midway between the Crags. As irrefutable proof of this story, the stone is there to this very day, about 20 tons of it, with the marks of the comb upon it still.

It is a very strong legend here that the whole of Arthur's court lies entranced in a cave beneath Sewingshields Castle, only to be awakened from their doom by (a) someone finding them, (b) drawing a sword from its scabbard and cutting the garter lying beside it and (c) blowing the bugle horn. The farmer at Sewingshields in the 18th century completed the first two requisites but was in such a sweat that he forgot to blow the horn with the result that the whole court reverted to its trance; as for the farmer, terror brought on loss of memory so he could never afterwards recall the exact venue. The vaulted remains of Sewingshields Castle, north-east of the present farm, were standing 5ft high in 1807, but were later removed and the whole area ploughed over.

Cross small plantation via the two stiles at each end, then continue due west past the stell and along to a gate and stile in field wall.

Inset: *Looking south at Cuddy's Crags from Pennine Way*

Left are Housesteads Crags where you get a tremendous impression of the height and impregnability of the Wall defences. They look strangely uninviting rocks, yet rowans and small shrubs find a foothold in them. Rowans, or mountain ash, grow higher up in Britain than any other species. Those clinging to the crevices have sprung from seeds dropped by birds who have been eating the berries. Another name for the rowan is the 'fowler's service tree' because huntsmen used its berries for baiting birds. It is called the rowan because of the colour of the berries, a rich scarlet in autumn, and it comes from the Gaelic — rudha-an: the red one.

Cross Pennine Way stile and continue along track to limekiln.

Rowan leaves and berries.

View west from Clew Hill

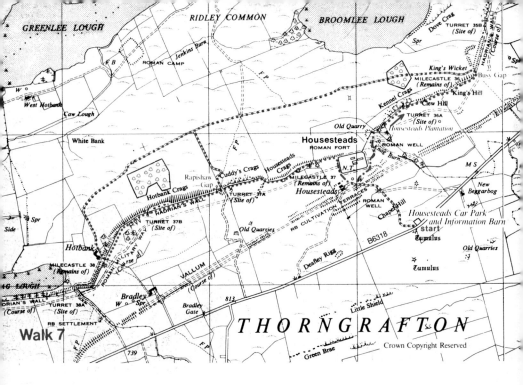

Walk 7

THORNGRAFTON

Crown Copyright Reserved

The ridge you have been walking along has long been a track between Hotbank and King's Wicket, probably part of a drove road with a track branching off northwards over Ridley Common to join up with Simonburn.

Limekilns alongside Pennine Way

At the limekiln continue west to Hotbank or, for a shorter walk, turn left and rejoin Wall at Rapishaw Gap (route description continues at page 44).

The limekiln, still well preserved, was well sited for ease of transporting the lime and coal. Also, you can see clearly from this one the way limekilns work. They are always built into a hill with the oven door at the base of the stone facing. The lime and coal was fed in from the top and raked out at the bottom in its final form.

Continue walking west on track past another stell to Hotbank Farm.

This stell is cross-shaped, which gives shelter whichever way the wind is blowing. Most of the sheep on this walk are Scottish Blackface, a very hardy breed. Crossed with a Border Leicester tup they produce mules — hybrid stock with no horns which fatten well for meat.

As you approach Hotbank Farm, Crag Lough, the second largest of the lakes, comes into view with the crags behind it and the Whin Sill climbing higher and higher to Winshields Crags.

Looking west towards Crag Lough from Hotbank Farm

At Hotbank Farm go through gate and across the farm yard and over stile to rejoin line of Wall. Turn left to walk east with Hadrian's Wall on left hand side.

Hotbank Farm is now owned by the National Trust. In 1704 it was owned by William Lowes who gave evidence against the Armstrongs of Housesteads for stealing sheep from his common.

Once past hexagonal wood stop on Hotbank Crags, 1,074ft above sea level. Four loughs are visible from here: Greenlee, the largest, Broomlee, Crag and Grindon, the smallest. These are shallow lakes, never more than about 10ft deep, formed by water being trapped in the slight depressions left by glacial erosion during the last Ice Age. In the 18th century to the south of Greenlee Lough and joined to it by a small burn, was 'Little Cow Lake'. At some time this area, which even then was full of reeds, has dried up and is now called Caw Lough, one of the 17 mires in the area and a Site of Special Scientific Interest.

On the crags at the south shore of Greenlee, at a height of 790ft, is an ancient semi-circular earth work, probably ancient British. Inside or close by are 15 shielings. They lie just within the parish of Thorngrafton and must therefore have been the summer pasturing places for people of that parish. The huts were quite large, 18-32ft long and 10-15ft wide, and

Crag Lough

some had an inside partition. There was also a temporary Roman camp at the south side of the lough, at West Hotbank.

Broomlee Lough, like Crag Lough, is stocked each year for fishing. According to legend, treasure is buried in its depths, sunk there long ago by a Lord of Sewingshields. It can be recovered only by using two twin yands (horses), two twin oxen, two twin lads and a chain forged by a smith of the kind (one who is seventh of his family in unbroken succession to have been smiths). One man is said to have nearly achieved this feat: he located the treasure, attached the chain and, using all the correct 'equipment' started the slow haul out. All went well until, at the crucial moment, a link in the chain snapped — and gone for ever was his chance to get rich quick.

Also visible from the heights of Hotbank Crags is Barcombe Hill to the south, where the Romans quarried stone for the Wall; they also took stone from Queen's Crags north of Sewingshields. To the south-west lie Cross

Hadrian's Wall looking east from Cuddy's Crags

Fell and Cold Fell of the Pennine range and on a clear day, Skiddaw and Saddleback in the Lakelands.

Continue east.

This part of the Wall is still the Pennine Way which, however, turns off left at Rapishaw Gap. After Rapishaw Gap come Cuddy's Crags, probably the most photographed and well known section of the whole Wall. Cuddy is a pet name for Cuthbert so, as St Cuthbert is the patron saint of Northumberland, the crags were probably named after him. During the Viking incursions into Northumberland, St Cuthbert's body was carried on horseback all over the County by the monks to escape the invaders, until they were able to lay his body to rest in Durham. It is from this period that the local name for a horse — 'cuddy' — is supposed to have come.

The gap at the east end of Cuddy's Crags is a particularly good example of a glacial cutting; it is about 50 yards wide and comes at a section where the ice has found a weakness in the rock and forced its way through on its way southwards. This action has occurred in numerous places all along the Whin Sill as you may have noticed when you descended one gradient only to have to climb up the next.

The Military Way is clear all along this stretch and is easily seen because the field gates are all placed on its route. In Roman times it was like a village street with houses lining it west of the fort of Housesteads. It was used as a pack road well into the last century when rather than follow the whole length of Wade's Military Road, the carriers used to branch off to the quieter and more gently graded Military Way.

About half way along Housesteads Crags is Milecastle 37 (Housesteads Milecastle). This is one of the best preserved milecastles with its north wall standing to above 10ft. It was built early in the Wall's construction by the second legion under Aulus Plautus Nepos, Hadrian's lieutenant up here.

Follow path to outskirts of Housesteads Fort. Walk between the fort and the museum to rejoin track back to car park.

8 Vindolanda - Henshaw; return via Chineley Burn

3½ miles, about 3 hours. A walk through fields, side roads and a village back up to Vindolanda via the Chineley Burn. The route at the end goes through the grounds of Vindolanda museum, adjacent to the excavated site so this walk can be extended to a full day's expedition if you wish to visit Vindolanda. It ends on the Stanegate, the Roman road linking Corbridge with Carlisle. Strong shoes are adequate for this walk unless the weather is wet in which case wellingtons are recommended.

Park at main Vindolanda car park.

Vindolanda fort covering 3½ acres lies south-east of the car park — you can see the reconstructions of wooden and stone turrets — on a natural platform, strong on all sides but the west. As a Stanegate fort it probably dates back to the early 80s AD, but underwent several rebuildings before being finally abandoned in the late 4th century. West of the camp was the civilian settlement (vicus), which included a bath house and married quarters. It was self-governing, providing labour for building the Wall and services for the Roman garrison: blacksmiths, carpenters, armourers, farriers etc. were all needed, and sometimes they sent their sons to join the occupying army.

Turn left on leaving car park by main exit and walk 100 yards to fingerpost sign. Turn left through gate.

The raised rectangular section of land to the left of the road is the site of a former farmhouse, Archie's Flat.

Walk south on track across field to gate into lonnen and up Kingcairn Hill.

wn Copyright Reserved

Look back and see Causeway Farm on the north side of the Stanegate. It has a noticeably steep pitch to the roof because at one time it was thatched. Heather was the multi-purpose thatching material, although turfs were also used.

This lonnen to Kingcairn Hill is part of a long track coming down from the Military Road to join up with Henshaw and the A69. As in all sunken lanes wild flowers grow in profusion: dog violet and primrose in the spring under the hedges and later on, honeysuckle, briar rose, and foxglove which attracts large numbers of bumblebees.

At junction of track with road carry straight on, south down tarmac road.

The recently closed Ramshaw Field Colliery lying 500 yards to the right was one of a number of small privately owned pits in the area selling coal locally. Older workings can be seen all the way down the field on the right of the wall in the next stretch of road; these were 'day pits' where a man took out what he could safely extract without props, and then moved on to another outcrop.

Where road bends round to left, go straight on following road sign to Henshaw.

Huntercrook plantation at the left corner of the junction is composed mostly of Scots pine and beech, making a fine shelter for the field beyond. Coal outcropped here too and more old pit workings appear on the southern edge of the wood.

The road you are now on has wide verges full of gorse and broom, honeysuckle and roses; locally it is still called 'Wet Lonnen', as before it was tarred it was a very wet, muddy lane. It is a marvellous place for picking brambles.

The beech trees in the high banks on each side, almost touching overhead, make this a

Women's Institute Hall, Henshaw.

magnificent avenue, rich with flowers — including wild raspberries. One beech, left, has an oak twined around its trunk.

At Huntercrook turn right past Brownside House. Just past Primrose House turn left to leave road through metal gate to Henshaw Hall.

Here is one of the best views over the South Tyne Valley: Willimoteswick and Langley Castles, the 100ft chimney on Langley Moor to carry off the fumes from the mills where lead ore was smelted, and beyond, the North Pennines.

Henshaw Hall is shortly going to revert to its old name, Waugh's Bank.

Walk left around house and over stone stile in wall. Follow field boundary (L), cross fence by stile, then over a second stone stile. A gate at the far end of this field leads into Henshaw Village.

Henshaw village itself is small but the parish stretches from the Tyne in the south to beyond the wastes of Scotchcoultard in the north; Melkridge and Thorngrafton parishes bound it on the west and east respectively. It was first mentioned in the 12th century when it was held by Richard Cumin and his wife Hextilda, descendant of King Duncan of Scotland who was murdered by Macbeth. Later it came into the possession of the Ridleys, perhaps the largest family in the district, based at Willimoteswick Castle, and then the Blacketts who were great coal owners. Henshaw parish produced substantial amounts of coal, including a seam 4ft thick in Scotchcoultard Waste and one 16in thick at Gallowshieldrigg.

In the village the single stone at the edge of the green is the only piece remaining of the bastle house that stood here — Hole Head.

Two-storey building with heather thatch at Henshaw. 1890's

47

With the ground floor for cattle and stone steps going up outside to the upper story where the family lived, this was pulled down early this century; some of the stones were built into the house called 'South View'. The Green is common land and must therefore remain unfenced. One attempt to enclose it was foiled when the young men of the village dismantled overnight the fencing that had been put up all round.

Many of the houses used to be single storied, thatched cottages and generally, by looking at the pitch of the roof and the structure of the upper story, it is possible to tell which have been altered. The old school was once a tithe barn and is now divided into two cottages.

Follow the road past the two chapels and walk to the road junction.

Methodism was strong in this area especially amongst the mining community. Here are two chapels side by side and there is another down the road. The Anglican church, All Hallows, built in 1888, is south of the village.

Cross road to wicket gate at back of chapel, now the Women's Institute Hall. Then follow FP along field edge. There are four more wickets between here and the farm road. The path goes by the side of each field so keep closely to it.

Nearly at the end of the second field take a look to the left of the path: sour dockens grow here — supposedly very good in sandwiches. You could risk trying one, with lots of butter and well seasoned with pepper and salt. Nettles can be included if you like.

Notice the way in which the trees of the old field boundary have been used in the more modern wall by the third wicket.

Chesterholme grounds from the footpath

After the fourth wicket the Red Burn comes down from the side of the field and in the wet ground marsh marigolds grow. This plant has attracted many regional names ranging from king cup to may blob. The local name in this area is water gollums.

The road is the A69, the main route between Newcastle and Carlisle. Originally built in 1752 and running between Corbridge and Haltwhistle, it was known as the Glenwhelt to Shildon Turnpike and later as the Hexham Turnpike until it was incorporated in the A69. Much of it, like the Military Road built only a year earlier, used Roman foundations. These roads made a big contribution to improving conditions in this region, both in maintenance of law and order and in promoting trade.

Marsh marigold

Cross farm road: go into field by wicket. Climb the hill keeping to the left, go through gate and cross stone stile at Parkside Farm. Keep farm buildings on left follow track and go through gate at end. Climb field path up to next gate.

To the left of the path are a few stones which show through the grass in a line up the field. These are part of a small stone-lined underground drain (cundy) which takes the water from a syke at the top of the field. Drainage is much less laborious now; plastic piping is used, laid in long continuous stretches.

After gate turn right down road for about 200 yards. Cross into field (L) by stone stile at bend in road.

A faint depression in the ground marks the old cart track which ran all the way down from High Fogrigg, by the Chineley Burn. Rough in places, more than one delivery cart in its time tipped over spilling its contents.

Cross field diagonally on ancient cart track heading for electricity pylon. The FP then goes directly north high above the Chineley Burn.

The ancient Britons lived on Barcombe Hill, the Romans found freestone for their Wall there and had a signal station at the north end linking Vindolanda with the east and west; more recently coal has been extracted. The four concrete blocks at the side of the footpath are the remains of an aerial flight which, using overhead cables, brought coal from the pit further up the burn, down to the railway siding at Bardon Mill. It was an attempt, 50 years ago, to by-pass the traditional carting of coal, but didn't last long because the pits closed.

Mining took place all over this area; spoil heaps are evident on the right of the burn, and to the left of the footpath below Low Fogrigg have suffered considerable subsidence from the mining activity underneath.

At Low Fogrigg (locally pronounced 'Fogridge') a bridge spans the Bean Burn just before its entry into the Chineley Burn; previously the ford was the only crossing. Cross the bridge and follow the path past Low Fogrigg up to the terrace above.

Across on the Barcombe side of the burn there used to be the colliery building. Here the miners kept their tokens. They collected them before they went down the pit and put them back at the end of the shift; if a token was missing a search was immediately put in hand for the missing miner.

At the top of the track the ground opens out to pasture surrounded by oak trees, about 200 years old. On the grassland skylarks and meadow pipits breed, and wood pigeons (known locally as cushats) come down to feed.

Go through wicket gate and follow the path to a small step over stile in the fence.

At the ruin, look across to Barcombe Hill, dominated by heather and a favourite site for adders and common lizards; they like to bask on rocks and paths in spring sunshine. Few walkers are ever troubled by adders, which detect the vibration of boots long before they are trodden on.

After stile walk on to meet museum boundary fence. Once across by step stile the path is waymarked. Turn right, follow burn and cross white bridge. The path goes round the side of the grounds and emerges at the Stanegate.

You can if you wish leave the path here to visit the museum.

Chesterholme, also called Little Chesters or The Bowers, was built in 1830 by the Rev. Anthony Hedley, a keen antiquarian who displayed many of the statues and stones he found in his excavations in the lovely grounds.

When the underground vaulting (the 'hypercaust') of the Roman baths in the fort were discovered 200 years ago, the stones blackened with soot, the local people were convinced that this was the kitchen to the palace of the Faery Queen!

Excavations are always exciting and the Vindolanda site is well worth visiting.

Leave Vindolanda by wicket gate beside cattle grid and turn left. Track leads past Codley Gate Farm.

The Stanegate runs along the right side of this road, joining up with it just north of the main fort. The track used to be, and still is locally called the Causeway — hence the name 'Causeway Farm' further along. Just after the bridge over the Brackies Burn, on the right with a tumulus behind it, is the only Roman milestone left standing intact in its original position — 200 years ago there were several.

Go past Codley Gate and back to the car park.

Codley Gate Farm on The Stanegate. Roman milestone on right. 1920's

9 Brocolitia - Teppermoor - Uppertown - Tecket; return via Kirkshield

3¾ miles, about 2¼ hours. Easy going over fields, through woods and along a drove road.

Park at Brocolitia car park. Turn right on leaving and walk 400 yards along Military Road to take BDWY marked 'to Uppertown': cross here and take care because traffic along this stretch is often dangerously fast.

Wade's road here, as on many lengths, is built right on top of Hadrian's Wall. In 1745 Bonnie Prince Charlie's forces came to Carlisle on their journey south. General Wade, commanding the King's forces and stationed at Newcastle, was balked of his prey at this point because there was no road between Newcastle and Carlisle fit to take his artillery. He had to wait and go south to intercept the Prince. Accordingly, just as the Romans had used this narrowest section of the country to build their coast-to-coast frontier, so did General Wade direct that a road be built here as the fastest route between east and west. It has ever since been called Wade's Road or the Military Road. Miles and miles of the Wall were flattened to form the base of the road (it had to be strong enough to take military traffic). The road building started in 1751; there were complaints at the time from antiquarians, but the plans went ahead and travellers ever since have blessed General Wade for providing them with such a splendid route. He actually died before it was started.

Follow BDWY 200 yards to High Teppermoor Farm.

The National Park starts just west of Tower Tye so Teppermoor has been able to take advantage of the National Park's small woods grants to plant hedgerow trees, supplementing the mature sycamores already there. The farm itself is largely built of stone from Hadrian's Wall. One modern addition is the silage clamp to the right, the three-sided wooden structure with a concrete base. Silage was first introduced into this country in the 1880s but it was only after World War II that farmers began to invest in silos on a big scale. They conserve the goodness in the grass very efficiently and remove the risk of summer rains spoiling the drying process so crucial in hay making. In 1776 Hutchinson had some hard words to say about Northumbrian hay making methods: 'the improvidence of the people in Northumberland touching their hay, is singular; it is put together in several heaps, or as they are called there, pikes, in the field where it is won, and stands in that form for many weeks before it is gathered into the mowe to stock; by which negligence much is wasted in the bottoms and outsides of the pikes'. Even now, with much better methods of hay making, a bad summer can spell doom and gloom to the farmer, with the result that more farmers are including silage as a crop.

At end of track cross the stile. Turn right

View north from footpath to Uppertown

at end of buildings and make for the nearer of the two gates (waymarked).

Moles are often busy in these fields, their underground runs throwing up soil heaps that cause problems for farmers. So they are trapped in large numbers, but it takes a professional mole-catcher to outwit a mole. Worms laced with strichnine are sometimes used as bait; or traps are used.

After gate follow stone-based track to next gate diagonally across the field.

By the gate there is a splendid collection of gate posts: you can see clearly how the brackets were set into the stone with lead.

Follow track on left side of the old wood, to the far end of the field.

The trees here provide a pleasant shelter for the stock, but the beasts graze not only the grass but the seedlings as well, so the trees do not regenerate. Eventually the wood will

die; meanwhile the trees play host to a number of lichens. These are formed by a fungus and an algae working together. They grow well on trees, buildings and gravestones, among other things, and while Wallis, curate of Simonburn in the 17th century, and a keen naturalist, counted 40 different lichens in the vicinity, there are about 1,355 species in Britain as a whole. Lichens have no roots but absorb moisture and gases through their exposed surfaces; consequently they are sensitive to atmospheric pollution and don't grow much in cities.

At field boundary turn left and walk alongside the wall to the ladder stile.

Just before the stile are a lot of rushes surrounding a pond and the wooden hides set around it. These are for duck shooting. At the stile, stop and look at the view. There is Chipchase Castle straight ahead; built in the

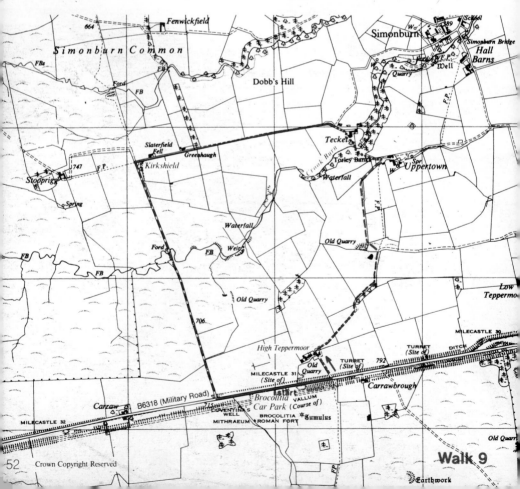

 Crown Copyright Reserved

Walk 9

14th century, it was the stronghold of the Heron family until it was bought by the Reeds of Redesdale, who built on the Jacobean front in about 1621. Closer is Park End, the seat of the Ridleys, once of Willimontswick; and in the far distance, on a clear day, you can see the Cheviot Hills.

Walk down the steep path to the stile at the bottom. Climb over and follow track, keeping field boundary on right.

The hedgerow trees here are mostly ash and sycamore; both are probably self-set, but whilst the former is the natural tree of limestone soils, the latter is an introduction from Europe. At the third tree down after the gate is a good cross-section of the dry stone wall showing the building technique to perfection: a tapering double row of stones with through stones ('thruffs'), rubble core and copings.

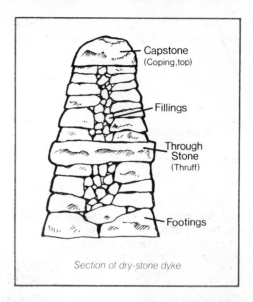

Section of dry-stone dyke

Stone culvert near Uppertown Farm

Follow this track through gate and at second gate turn right to Uppertown.

Just before the gate the wall bridges a small syke that runs down the side of this field. Once through the gate look to the right and you will see the bridging from the other side and also a small channel built at right angles for another trickle of water from the adjoining field. Then see the way the water has been channelled under the track —skilled stone work.

Kingcups and water mint grow by the sides of the syke. The track to Uppertown is enhanced by a lovely avenue of trees, and at the far end is a fascinating collection of old farm implements and machinery.

Just before the buildings at Uppertown turn left at the ivy-clad ruin and on to cart track.

The ruin gives a good foothold to various plants including foxglove, ivy and the polypody fern.

Go through gate across farm track then enter the wood via wicket gate. Follow track down to footbridge over the Crook Burn.

Some felling of spruce and dead trees has recently taken place in the wood but the magnificent beeches remain; it is thought they were planted in the 1740s. A short way down the track is a massive rock that looks as if it is hurtling to the burn below. There are a lot of massive rock falls in these woods, possibly due to an earth tremor — there was one in 1880.

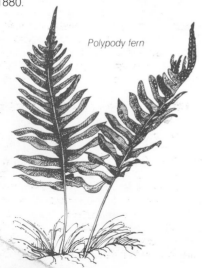

Polypody fern

Boulder in wood near Crook Burn

Cross the footbridge and climb bank opposite (waymarked).

There are blackthorn bushes on this bank; its fruit is the sloe, greatly prized by sloe gin enthusiasts.

The Tecket Farm is at the top. This was listed in the 1542 survey of border strongholds as a strong house but it is not known when it was built. When alterations were carried out on it a few years ago massive walls and an archway were found inside. It was owned by the Ridleys in the 17th century and they sold it to the Giles Heron Trust in about 1690. Giles Heron was the natural son of a Heron of Chipchase. An itinerant pedlar, he carried souples, for making flails, to sell in Scotland. He was a man of extreme parsimony, begging his dinner rather than pay for it, gathering wisps of hay left on the hedgerows rather than pay for any for his horse, and at his death had saved £800. His will dated 1683 directed that the money be used to found a free school in Wark for the children of the parish of Simonburn, of Birtley, Birtley Shields and Chipchase. He also provided for the relief of the poor in the parish of Simonburn and for the binding of apprentices, always those with the surname 'Heron' to have precedence.

Turn left where the track joins the metalled road and walk up here to Kirkshield.

It is very bleak up this stretch; even a moderate fall of snow can block the road for days because the land is so exposed, and then it is often easier to get out over the fields. Slaterfield Fell on the right, with its granary still intact, was once owned by the Ridleys. Kirkshield, on the left, also known as the 'Folly', was built in the 17th century by a rector of Simonburn as a shooting lodge. In the 18th century the rector had an income of £5,000 per annum; his curate, the historian Wallis, had £30 per annum.

Turn left at end of road on track leading south to Military Road.

This is an old drove road which comes down from the north leading southwards to the Military Road. The right hand side is bounded by hawthorn and an old dry stone dyke. The line of the road is particularly well defined with its wide verges, after the second stile. A drove road is an ancient, unmetalled track along which cattle were driven when they had to be moved, for example, to and from market. People remember flocks of geese being driven along this road, and it was this route that the farmer's wife from Stooprigg (half a mile north of here) used to follow every week, with two enormous market baskets on her arm, one full of eggs and one full of butter and heading for the mart at Hexham. She had to walk down to Fourstones (about 5 miles) catch the train there into Hexham, sell her goods and then make the return trip.

At the bottom of the field is the Crook Burn; fresh-water crayfish, like miniature lobsters about 4in long, live under the flat stones in the bottom. They only live in streams with a well oxygenated water supply and even then prefer ones in limestone districts. As evidence of a limestone presence there is a limekiln to the left of the next stile.

After the second stile the ground becomes rougher. Fozy Moss is to the right, one of the 17 important mire sites in the Hadrian's Wall area. The conditions suit curlew and lapwing, and you may set up a bevy of partridge.

At the Military Road turn left and walk back to car park taking care to walk on the right hand side of the road.

If you have time, take a look at Carrawburgh fort (Brocolitia) and the Mithraic Temple, both served by the car park.

The fort is quite grown over but its siting right across the line of the vallum is clearly visible. Built after the Wall it measures 360ft east-west and 460ft north-south. It has been excavated several times but the most memorable discovery was the treasure of Coventina's Well, just west of the field wall. Clayton, who had long known of the well but who thought it was nothing extraordinary, excavated it in 1876 and found not just a heap of stones at the top but a mass of coins, masonry, jewelry, incense burners, votive objects left as offerings, all apparently hurled into the well in a panic. Altogether 13,487 coins were recovered, 4 gold, 184 silver and the rest bronze dating from Mark Anthony to Gratian. 327 of the bronze coins dated from the pacification of Northern Britain after the disturbances of AD 155 and these show Britannia, not as the proud lady on the backs of some of our coins, but as a dejected, rumpled figure, sitting on a rock, chin in hand, banner lowered and shield cast aside.

Below the fort is the Mithraic Temple, now in the guardianship of The English Heritage. This was discovered in 1949 and a full-scale reconstruction of the earliest Mithraeum, with commentary, is in the Museum of Antiquities in Newcastle.

The Military Road in the 1890's looking west from a position near the present day Brocolitia car park

The South Tyne area

The last four walks are outside the National Park, south of the River South Tyne. Historically the story is much the same: Hadrian's Wall is not in the immediate vicinity, but it is still on the horizon; Roman troops were stationed nearby and Roman roads intersected the land. The inhabitants had the same defence problems during the Border Wars as their neighbours north of the river: Featherstone Castle (Walk 10), Bellister Castle (Walk 11) and Staward Peel (Walk 12) bear witness to this.

A good proportion of the walks lie in the valley bottoms where the shifting course of the River Tyne, by its movements over the centuries, has created rich haughlands, and arable farming is supported as well as the stock rearing of the higher ground.

It is still limestone country with rich coal deposits, especially where the land rises to the moors in the south. The Allen gorge, gouged out during the last Ice Age and deepened by the action of its fast flowing river, reveals some impressive coal strata along its banks. It also supports some of the oldest woodlands in the country near Briarwood Banks. These are not in the walks but form one of the Northumberland Wildlife Trust's Nature Reserves and can be visited.

The River Allen

57

10 Featherstone footbridge - Lambley Farm; return via Featherstone Park

3½ miles, about 2½ hours. A riverside and woodland walk with a wide variety of birds and plant life. The ground is often very wet so wellingtons or boots are advised except in the driest of summers.

Park just downstream from the footbridge over the South Tyne, GR 673613. Cross the stile and footbridge.

The stone piers which support the footbridge are covered with lichens and there are also beautiful mosses growing in the undercut sides of the bank to the right of the path. On the south side of the river the bank has been built up. The Tyne is particularly prone to change course and this sort of work is necessary if the bank isn't to be eroded

altogether. Slightly upstream is a gauging station built by the Northumbria Water Authority in the 1960s. This records the speed at which the South Tyne rises and falls; it also has a warning system so that if major flooding is developing people downstream can be warned, and the new dam at Riding Mill adjusted to cope with the extra flow. The gauging station also includes a salmon leap. Just below is a pool where the fish can rest so that if they fail at their first jump they can have a second go.

Featherstone Bridge, 700 yards downstream from the start of the walk, was built in the 1760s

They shouldn't have too much difficulty here because a large adult salmon can leap about 11ft.

Turn left and walk along riverside path.

Because of its dampness the right bank is full of ferns, liverwort (so called because it resembles the lobes of the liver) and mosses. A dry waterfall here is evidence of drainage but because of constant flooding and the seep of moisture from the steep banks, the earth will constantly be wet enough to support these colonies. While some mosses will grow in quite dry, stony places, the liverwort needs a damp atmosphere so that its delicate leaves don't dry up.

You can now see Featherstone Castle clearly on the other side of the river.

Featherstone first appears in Henry III's reign as a Manor in the Barony of Langley, held by a Featherstone and thereafter in unbroken succession for twelve generations. In the 1542 survey of border strongholds Featherstone was 'in good reparations'. The oldest part (13th century) is nearest the road; it was restored in the 14th century, and after the union of the crowns in 1603 and the gradual peace that came to the borders, extensive reconstruction of the castle took place. The castle, haunted by a ghostly bridal party, is perhaps the most attractive of all the border strongholds.

The Featherstones were an important family on the borders: Thomas was bailiff of Tynedale and Steward of the Barony of Langley in Henry III's reign. His son Thomas was keeper of Staward Peel (see Walk 12), which he rebuilt. He had the duty of selecting men fit for military service in the liberties of Hexham, Wark and Tynedale. In Henry VIII's reign Richard was chaplain and manager for Catherine of Aragon, the first divorced wife of the King, and such was his zeal for her cause that in 1542 he was executed. As for Albany Featherstonehaugh, High Sheriff of Northumberland in 1530, he is immortalised in the ballads:

Hoot awa', lads, hoot awa',
Ha ye heard how the Ridleys, and Thirlwalls, and a',
Ha' set upon Albany Featherstonehaugh
And taken his life at the Deadmanshaw?

Actually, this was a spoof ballad by Robert Surtees and sent as a joke to Sir Walter Scott who was completely taken in by it. All these legends and ghost stories are part of the tradition of Northumberland. In a land much battered by warfare, where the population was widely scattered with little education or

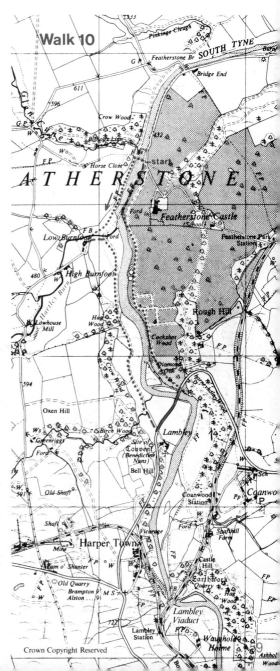

entertainment, a rich vein of folklore was handed down by word of mouth over generations — it was one of the major sources of entertainment in the long dark winters — and fortunately many of the ballads were saved by being collected and written down. But a true Northumbrian was ever a superb story teller; and the taller the story the better.

The path now leaves the side of the river and goes across the haughland towards Low Burnfoot Farm. A concrete/metal footbridge takes you over the Hartley Burn. Turn sharp left and follow burn side to open fields. Turn right into field and cross to far corner (heading south). Climb stile at end of field and follow waymarking.

The land here has been farmed for centuries but always grazed, never cropped — too difficult of access.

The ground here is like a primeval swamp. Try to keep to the path where drainage work has been carried out. The area of haughland which you have now reached is known as Madam's Island.

At end of field cross stile by hawthorn hedge.

The farmer here at Lambley Farm keeps Southdown sheep. Normally, Cheviots, Border Leicesters and Blackfaced are the breeds most favoured in the area. These Southdowns however are good for fattening and have a fine fleece. The hope is that they will be able to lamb three times in two years. If they do, helped by better feedstuffs, they will make a very useful crop.

The path continues through two gates. On reaching Lambley Farm pass through the wicket gate and turn left onto new road bridge.

This bridge was opened in 1976 as part of the new road from Alston to Haltwhistle to replace the railway line. Lambley Viaduct a few

British Railways NER Class G5 No.67241 leaving Lambley Station on the Haltwhistle to Alston route. Lambley Viaduct in the background. About 1952-3

...atherstone Castle from the riverside path

hundred yards upstream, is the most outstanding feature of the Haltwhistle to Alston Railway. A branch line of the Newcastle to Carlisle line, it opened in 1852 with a branch off from Lambley to Halton Lea Gate, the Lambley Fell Branch. It served both passengers and goods from Alston, the highest market town in England, and closed only after much opposition in 1976. The National Park Authority plans to create a public right of way along it to the boundary with Cumbria at Gilderdale.

Just beyond Lambley Farm and marked with a cross on the map, was the Benedictine convent founded by Adam de Tindale and Heloise his wife in the 12th century. Religious communities, like the Romans, were always good at choosing their sites. This one, with an ample supply of water, good grazing, in a picturesque setting well protected from the north wind, fell victim to a brutal raid by the Scots in 1296; the house was burnt, the countryside ravaged and atrocities committed on the nuns. The convent was restored and at the dissolution of the monasteries in Henry VIII's reign six nuns resided there. The house was still standing in 1599 but the River Tyne, even then, was washing through its walls. Every vestige has long since been swept away by the river.

Cross road bridge and turn left through gate to follow track running parallel with river.

This is Featherstone Park, beautifully laid out in the 18th and 19th centuries. Oystercatchers often nest on the gravel islands. These are noisy wading birds with bold black and white plumage and a heavy red beak. On the seashore these birds feed on cockles, but inland, during the breeding season, they have taken to eating earthworms, and this newly-

German POWs enacting a play at Featherstone Castle in 1947

acquired habit has enabled them to colonise further and further up the river valleys.

Right of the bridleway are the remains of the Featherstone Park Prisoner of War Camp, used as a transit camp in World War II.

Featherstone Park was chosen because of its situation close to a rail-head and because it offered few chances of escape. As witness to this only nine men ever tried to get away: eight went for the river but when one drowned mid-stream, the others returned to camp. The ninth man got as far as Haydon Bridge, hiding on the back of a truck. He jumped out to get to the railway, but got to the arms of the local bobby instead.

100 huts housed up to 7,000 prisoners at any one time while they were de-loused, re-clothed, sorted out according to trade and sent on to permanent workcamps elsewhere; 200 British troops guarded them.

After D-Day German POWs came here and in the freer post-war atmosphere were allowed to associate with the local community, working on the farms, and doing odd jobs in the area. They also had their own newspaper, 'Die Zeit am Tyne' printed for them in the local press offices at Hexham. For the people of Haltwhistle it has been a matter of pride that when the camp closed an Association was set up by an officer from the camp to foster better understanding between England and Germany. Contact has been maintained with the ex-prisoners and this has continued into the next generation.

The FP continues past Featherstone Castle.

Featherstone Castle is still very much lived in. During two world wars it was used as a prep. school but is now privately owned.

Continue along river bank past metal footbridge to return to car.

Oystercatchers

Featherstone footbridge over the River South Tyne

11 Park Burnfoot - Park Village - Broom Houses; return via Bellister Castle

4 miles, about 3 hours. A walk away from the Wall, starts and finishes in woodland above the banks of the South Tyne and in between goes through Park Village and on to the high land with superb views over South Tyne and Allendale. Boots recommended, or wellingtons in wet weather.

Park at pull-in on left (south) of road just before Park Burnfoot Farm, GR 684620.

This farm is at the confluence of Park Burn and the South Tyne. The weir just upstream of the car park used to provide water power for Featherstone Park sawmill behind the farm.

Cross road, walk uphill for 50 yards (past campsite entrance) and enter wood via stile. Turn right and follow waymarked path.

This was part of the old road. The metalled one was made earlier this century. Bluebells in early summer and the honeysuckle and briar rose later on make this a very pretty start to the walk.

Emerging onto the road turn left then right at road junction and on to Park Village ahead. The new road bypasses the village but it is worth taking the old road to look at it.

Many of the houses are owned by the Bellister Estate, the oldest being dated 1711 and the latest, until recently, 1888. The uniformity of the stone is because most of it was brought from the stone quarry just south of the village; it was an Awarded Quarry (that is, it was given to the village for their use), so the stone was readily available in the village. The Snowdon family farmed in the village and the initial S appears over several doorways along with another initial and a date. The way of life in the last century in this area was crofting; beasts were pastured on the common land at Park Bents and the houses were built to accommodate them below stairs while the people lived above. The signs are there on a number of houses. The streets were cobbled — a few house fronts have them still — until an outbreak of cholera or typhoid (everyone said it was the Black Death) in the early 1900s was traced to the water supply. Open drains ran down the side of the street and the water was easily polluted. A proper sewage system

was put in as a result of this and the road metalled.

Leave the village by the bridge over the railway track.

Park Village's first Chapel was just to the left of this bridge. The railway company paid for it to be dismantled when they constructed this track and had the present one built. That was in the 1850s.

Regain main road at junction and turn right. Walk along here for 200 yards until turning left through gate at Park Bents. Follow farm track towards Linn Shield.

Park Bents was the common pasture for the

Low Burnfoot Farm

Park Village crofters. The name seems to derive from 'Park' for the village, while 'Bents' means a heath or unenclosed pasture. Bents is also another word for grass.

In the field to the right you may see lapwings (or peewits, so called because of their call) massing. They come here to feed — they like worms, but nest on higher, rougher ground with plenty of tussocks for protection. They never lay more than four eggs, browny green in colour with a speckled effect for camouflage, and the fledglings can run as soon as they emerge from the shell. They belong to the plover family and while plovers' eggs were considered (and still are) a great delicacy by some people, the lapwing was more commonly a prey to people for eating. They were caught by a decoy method. A tame lapwing, with a long piece of string attached to its leg, was placed in a likely field with a clap net beside it, and the hunters retreated to the shelter of hedge or wall, clasping the other end of the string. When a flock of wild lapwing came overhead, the huntsmen twitched the string, making the

Lapwing - also known as 'peewit'

tame bird flap its wings thus decoying the flock to come and investigate. At which point they were entrapped in the clap net. Very tasty; up to 50 years ago there was a considerable market in these small waders. In Spain they are called the 'storm bird', being seen there usually in stormy weather.

After cattle grid and just before next gate turn left and follow track keeping wall on right. Go through gate and follow track slowly uphill, bearing slightly left.

It is still relatively sheltered here, foxgloves grow in the lee of the wall, and the pasture is covered with daisies. The first part of the track is edged on the right by an old grass-covered stone dyke with holly trees, hawthorn and birch growing along its line.

The herring gull, white with grey wings, comes inland in winter to feed, but returns to the coast for nesting. They are often in the field on the left early in the year. Their habit of visiting inland sites is quite recent, following their discovery of the joys of free food on rubbish tips.

Pass through second gate and continue along field track.

The track is an old waggoners' way which links up with Broom Houses via Throstle Hall. It hasn't been used for decades, but is still very clearly marked; in some places the stone base shows through the grass. There are so many birds up here; chaffinch are active, but it is the thrush which predominates. This may be the reason why Throstle Hall got its name. The 'Hall' part is more of a mystery because it is really a very small cottage, as you will see when you get to it.

Go through third gate and continue towards Throstle Hall, on the right.

This is about the highest spot along this stretch and it's not very far from Hadrian's Wall country. Hopealone GPO mast, as always, is visible in Wark Forest; the Whin Sill and Barcombe Hill stand out to the north-east. The trees along here are very old — hawthorns, hollies and oaks along the boundary. The ground becomes wet before the next gate with a lot of rushes — always a sign of poorly drained land.

At the fourth gate a side track branches off left leading over the old railway. The roof of Throstle Hall can just be seen, ivy covered and ruined. The oak and ash are here

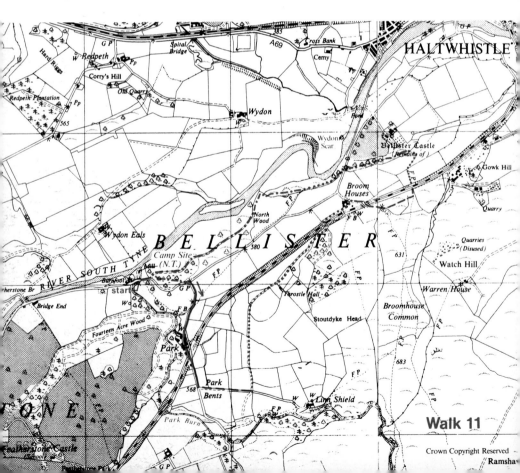

Walk 11

Crown Copyright Reserved
Ramsha

they wq the field edge, along with the holly, Graduïd hawthorn.

the **track passes to the left of the Hall** fa**tween two gate posts and carries on** **ownhill across the bottom field, the railway cutting on the left. Walk towards the gate at the far end of the field.**

The ground here is wet. A lake, in the bottom, had to be drained when the railway track was laid; a narrow stone channel runs along one side of the track to take the water off the fields. When you get to the gate, look at the left hand gate post; with its extraordinary markings it looks as though it has Roman origins.

Go through gate, follow path over railway bridge and turn right to Broom Houses.

In 1568 Broom Houses belonged to the Blenkinsopps of Bellister. It was sold along with the manor and tithes of Bellister to a William Ramsay of Newcastle in 1697 and by an Act of Parliament in 1775 they were sold by his descendants to Henry Ellison of Gateshead Park.

Leave Broom Houses by middle (waymarked) gate. Follow path back over railway. Pass through two metal gates across path then turn left through the next gate in wall. Turn right and walk on for about 200 yards along field top then left, downhill towards stiles, one on each side of railway track.

The factory complex further down beside the railway line is the Cascelloids Division of BXL Plastics Ltd. They make plastic bottles and started production in 1960.

Recross the railway by waymarked stiles. Second stile leads straight ahead to stone stile at top of hill. If field is used as hay meadow, single file please. After the stile, set off diagonally right, towards eastern (R) end of wood ahead.

This field affords the first close view of Bellister Castle. If there is a noise of an engine about to blow up don't worry, it's just the donkey braying in the farm yard! Bellister was built for the Blenkinsopps in the 15th century as a pele tower; that part is now in ruins. The inhabited part is the castellated farmhouse beside it. The castle is haunted by the Grey Man of Bellister. A wandering minstrel some centuries ago was turned out of the castle on suspicion of being a spy and afterwards hunted down by the castle's pack of bloodhounds. The fearsome beasts ran the old man to earth

under some willows by the river and there finished their grisly work. The minstrel since that day has haunted the tower, ever hopeful of wreaking his awful revenge.

The castle and grounds were left to the National Trust in 1979 and the pele tower can be visited by arrangement.

Arriving at the fence cross the step stile into the wood and follow the waymarking through it.

At first the wood is mixed with a number of naturalised rhododendrons. Once past the castle it is planted with beech, magnificent specimens towering above the sloping earth and providing a deep carpet of dried leaves. Not many other species grow in beech woods because dense leaf cover blots out the light in summer and in winter the slow decomposition of the leaves means that nothing very much can come through. On the other hand the

Bellister Castle from the footpath

Wren

sound of birds is everywhere, especially the tiny wren whose voice, in inverse proportion to its size, never seems to cease.

Leave wood by gate: cross road and enter wooded river bank. Follow waymarking

Park Burnfoot Cottage from across the Park Burn

(woodland walk).

This is newer woodland with a lot of conifers. The top banks look over the river and you can see clearly how the bed has shifted over the centuries. Wydon Scar, that high cliff seen on the far bank, is perhaps the best example of how this river has worn away its banks over the centuries. One of the reasons for there not being a road along the bottom of the South Tyne valley until the 1830s was the shifting nature of this river. It was only when the Newcastle to Carlisle railway was built that the river was straightened, constrained and generally kept in place. Even so it still moves a lot and if ever there is prolonged or heavy rain don't go near the river because it floods very easily.

Return to base via the National Trust camp site.

Opened in 1979 it caters largely for tented campers; already it is well used, particularly by those visiting Hadrian's Wall. There is also a small shop in the grounds which sells refreshments and National Trust literature.

12 Staward Station - Staward Peel - Plankey Mill; return via Sillywrea and Harsondale

5 miles, 3½ hours. A field, woodland and riverside walk of rare beauty - magnificent views, history, a wealth of flowers, some of the best woodlands in the County and everywhere teeming with birdlife and wild animals.

Park at pull-in on south side of A686 at junction with Allendale road, GR807597. Cross A686, enter field through metal gate, turn right and follow sunken track downhill to Gingle Pot, a ruined cottage.

Land use depends a lot on the prevailing economic pressures; during World War II when food supplies from overseas were short, this field and others like it were used for corn crops, mostly barley. Later (it is about 700ft above sea level) it reverted to rough pasture. The stone trough right of the path is vital for the stock when there is no natural water supply to the pasture.

The ruined cottage on the left is Gingle Pot. In its time a pub, it was also a useful stopping place for picnickers once the railway brought the countryside nearer to the people. Here they could always get hot water for their kettles — people picnicked in style in those days!

Go through gate and, keeping first the stone wall then the wood on your right, follow well-worn path straight ahead leading to corner of wood and stile.

The mainly coniferous wood to the right is the Forestry Commission's. Roe deer sometimes come to its edge and enter the field. Native to this country, they have a distinctive white patch on the rump, and are notoriously shy.

The pasture on the left has been extensively

View west across Allen gorge, near Plankey Mill

drained, but still the rushes grow. In early spring there is a lot of black sedge in this field sticking up above the grass; lady's smock, a mauve coloured bloom, grows here too. More often in evidence are the curlew and quite a number of pheasant and partridge. About 15-20 years ago the increasing use of chemical sprays almost led to the total destruction of the partridge, a native bird. Most estates put a ban on shooting them and actively protected them in other ways; now their numbers are increasing again and it is good to see them suddenly whirr away from beneath your feet. But it was a close run thing — the corncrake wasn't so lucky. Nesting in meadowland and cornfields the introduction of mechanised farming completely destroyed their traditional nesting grounds and, of course, their young. They are now restricted to meadowland in the north and west of Scotland and to Ireland. Seldom seen, the corncrake nevertheless has a very distinctive call — something like running the back of one's finger down a comb.

Cross stile into wood and follow path. You soon see that you are on a wooded ridge with steep drops on each side.

Immediately the flowers change: here are water avens, of the geum family, vetch and bugle in among the grasses. Further in, heather and bilberry indicate it is acid soil, while briar rose and honeysuckle grow in profusion amidst the hazel, birch and Scots

Water avens

pine. Further along the path there is a well-trodden platform on the right. Step aside here and look into the ravine: at the bottom of an almost vertical drop of 300ft is the Harsondale Burn. The path is the crest of a narrow ridge between this burn and the River Allen (left). Turn aside a few yards further on to have a look at that too.

The path now comes to the gateway to Staward Peel. This entrance, strengthened by drawbridge, portcullis and iron gate led to the pele tower now with walls left only 10ft high, built at the very point of this narrow tongue of land high above the Allen and Harsondale Burn. An almost impregnable stronghold constructed of dressed limestone, the whole was surrounded by a wall built on the very edge of the rock. Held by the Friars Eremites of Hexham and the Swinburnes, it was sold in the 14th century to Queen Phillippa. James I conveyed it in 1613 to Theophilus, Lord Howard of Walden and in 1664 it was sold for £450 to Mr Bacon. There were no trees here when the pele was built, so there would have been far more extensive views. Wood for repairs in the 15th century had to come from Bywell. Staward Wood was first planted in the 1790s — with Scots pine, beech, elm, sycamore, ash, poplar and sweet chestnut. After felling and replanting larch was added.

After Staward ruin follow narrow and steep winding path downhill bearing left to stone wall at bottom. Turn right, follow path to Harsondale Burn and cross by footbridge.

The overriding scent in spring time is garlic from the masses of ramsons growing beneath and between the trees and path. The footbridge crosses the burn just before its confluence with the River Allen. Upstream are massive boulders, some of them deposited by winter torrents and others fallen from the steep heights above. Almost perfectly square, stone like this must have been easy to win for building the pele.

Follow FP towards River Allen and walk along bank.

Flood water has cut deeply into the opposite bank exposing the limestone strata; coal is very evident. There is more downstream. Keep a look out for the common sandpiper along here, and the oyster catchers. Cuckoo

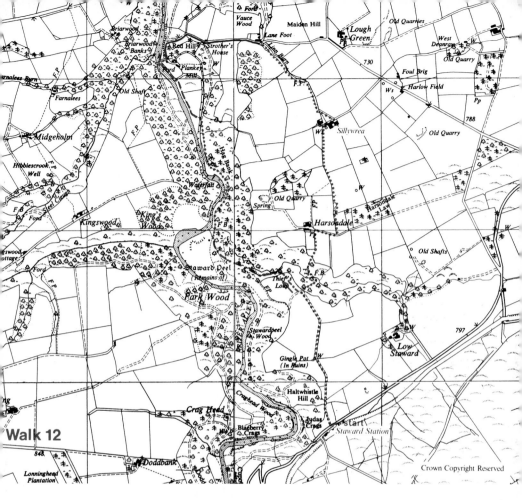

Walk 12

Crown Copyright Reserved

pint will probably be growing at some stage of its cycle, either with its wide leaves and hooded stamen spike in June/July or with its cluster of bright red berries in August. It likes wettish shady ground so this area is ideal. In times past people obtained arrowroot from the roots of this plant but some parts of it, particularly the berries, are poisonous. Something not to be missed slightly back from the path on the left, are some splendid yew trees. There is a first group of three and then another of nine or so. Conifers predominate from here to the end of the wood.

Leave wood by gate into meadow with Plankey Farm at the far end and continue alongside river to stile. Cross it and follow path between river and fence passing end of suspension bridge to road.

Yew leaves and berries

Plankey Mill has been a favourite picnic, swimming and camping spot for years. The Allen banks all the way down from Ridley Hall provide excellent walks, with a wide variety of plants, trees and wildlife. Briarwood Banks, a fragment of ancient woodland, is one of the Northumberland Wildlife Trust's nature reserves. The suspension bridge gives access to the left bank. The farm here is privately owned but the National Trust own the land on both sides of the river downstream from the old Plankey Mill.

Walk round back of old buildings on road.

Half way up the hill you can see the actual mill building and the mill race. About opposite is where the National Trust land starts.

Continue uphill on road past Strother's House to Lane Foot on left of road. Just past the house cross stile (R) alongside Linn Burn and follow field edge, through gates to Sillywrea Farm.

The sheep here are Cheviots and black faced Suffolk, both hardy breeds and good for fattening. The Suffolk in particular has a good fleece.

At farm turn right on farm road past arched hemel and through metal gate (L). Go uphill keeping stone wall on right and aim for stone stile in wall ahead.

Sillywrea is an odd name possibly meaning a place surrounded by trees, and is an old farm dating back at least to the 16th century. Mr Dodd who farms Sillywrea now believes that some of the older farming methods are best. He uses no tractors for his farmwork; rather he harnesses his Clydesdales to his

Plankey Mill suspension footbridge

machinery. It may take longer but he reckons it is better. You may have noticed some of the carts, ploughs and farm vehicles in the yard. He has three Clydesdales, probably running out on the field. Lean, hairy and big-boned horses capable of sustained work, they are the Scottish equivalent of the Yorkshire Shire horse, both descendants of the sturdy war horses that carried the extremely well armoured and therefore extremely heavy knights of old. As the soil here is a heavy clay the Clydesdales need to be sturdy.

At the top of the hill at 850ft look back to the north and see Winshields Crags in the far distance. Closer in is a limekiln, evidence that limestone is present in this area too, but not quite so much as in Hadrian's Wall country.

Go over stone stile into more pasture and head for beech trees, a shelter belt for the former cottage. Continue alongside fenced-off garden (now a potato patch). At end cross step stile (R), go across line of hawthorns to corner and cross wall by stone stile. Descend field and turn right after crossing stile next to gate. You are now on the Harsondale Farm road.

Harsondale Farm even older than Sillywrea, was mentioned in a deed dated 1302 and is at the end of the track. This has been farmed by one family, the Whites, for over 200 years.

Walk down track towards Harsondale Farm but just before farm buildings turn left over wooden stile and follow hedge line down the field to pass through wicket gate into wood. Go downhill through wood and cross footbridge to climb back up the other side.

This is a new bridge. The previous one had to be replaced when it was tipped to a dangerous angle by flood water. On the stone-work of the bridge, spleenwort and liverwort grow — the former in dry places and the latter on the damp, dark buttress. Along the burnside are several characteristic plants, including the blue-flowered brooklime, which rejoices in the latin name of Veronica beccabunga.

At top of slope the FP seems to disappear in a swamp: turn right into wood to avoid it and follow path up to gate into field below Gingle Pot and walk back up the fields to starting point.

Harsondale Farm

13 Haydon Bridge - Elrington; return via Threepwood

3½ miles, about 2 hours. A very attractive field and woodland walk on the south side of Haydon Bridge, suitable for all seasons.

Park at roadside bay on cemetery side of road, GR 843639. Cross to stile opposite parking bay. This leads into school playing field. Walk diagonally across towards school. At wall, turn right below trees until path joins the lane.

The Shaftoe Trust School at Haydon Bridge was founded by a deed of the Rev John Shaftoe, dated 1685. He appointed seven trustees and instructed that after his death they should use his estate of Mousen to pay for the building and subsequent funding of 'a free grammar school-house and [to] keep an English school'. The headmaster had to be 'a university scholar, of the degree of Master of Arts, and of good life and conversation'. Boys, girls and young men from the chapelries of Haydon and Woodshields, both in the parish of Warden, were to benefit from this. Furthermore, the usher, or undermaster, was not to be permitted to charge more than 1d a quarter for the 'teaching and instruction of them in the Latin and Greek tongues'.

After Shaftoe's death in 1697 the trustees, as instructed, bought three roods of ground on the Chapel Hill (apparently the old Chapel of Langley was here) and built a school and a school house. In 1785, due to the considerable increase in revenue from the estate of Mousen, an Act of Parliament was passed for the better regulation of the charity and a girls' school was added to teach reading, writing, arithmetic, knitting and so on. Further reorganisation in 1819 by the Charity Commissioners changed the school into an elementary school and it is now a County High School. That part of it is on the north bank of the village; this part here, which still bears the Shaftoe name, is the junior school. One particularly eminent ex-pupil was John Martin, the artist. He was born at East Lands Ends in 1789 and displayed early signs of genius. Rather than join his mates at playtime he stayed indoors sketching on his slate and drawing cartoons on the wall of his masters and fellow pupils. He left the region at 14 and a number of his paintings are now in the Laing Art Gallery in Newcastle — vast canvasses usually of classical or biblical themes.

After the school continue along lane past terraced houses towards the wood.

John Shaftoe's will also provided for almshouses for 20 poor persons. These make up Shaftoe Terrace. This John Shaftoe possibly from the same family as Bobby Shaftoe, that bonny lad who went to sea, with silver buckles on his knee.

Continue along lane and follow path into wood and over footbridge.

This is Gees Wood (pronounced with a hard G), predominantly oak, beech and chestnut, and has long been a favourite Sunday afternoon walk for Haydon Bridge people; with its trees, deep gorges and the Langley Burn running through, it is very attractive. In spring there are masses of bluebells which suggests that there has been woodland on this site for

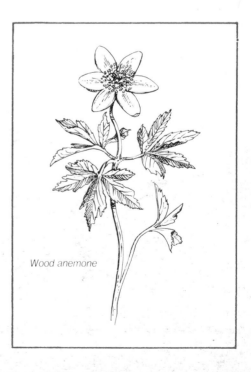

Wood anemone

many years, since they take a long time to establish themselves in new woods and are absent from softwood plantations. The flowering of 'vernal' (spring) plants, like the bluebell, anemone and celandine is synchronised with the leafing of the wood — the reproductive cycle is virtually finished when the summer darkness arrives. Softwoods like pine and spruce are always in leaf, so there is no light spring season for the flowers to grow.

The path climbs out of the wood and goes between a field (L) and a deep gorge (R).

This end of Gees Wood is now planted with a variety of spruce and beneath grow gorse and rosebay willowherb.

At the end of the path turn left onto A686. Cross the road and walk down its right hand side as far as the junction with A69.

View west from footpath near Elrington

Looking south you can see Haydon Bridge first mentioned in the 14th century; in 1323 Anthony de Lucy, Baron of Langley, procured a charter for a market and fair for the village. The bridge has always been an important crossing place; during the border warfares it was gated, this being constantly barred, chained and locked. There are two bridges now, one erected about 15 years ago carrying the road traffic, and the old one for pedestrians only.

The church, on the north side with the pagoda style roof to the tower, was built in 1796 on land provided by Greenwich Hospital, and is dedicated to St Cuthbert. The old Chapel of Haydon, high on the tops about ½ mile north of the village, is far older. Also dedicated to St Cuthbert, it was probably built in the 12th century. Surrounded by a large walled graveyard with ancient yew trees, it is very small, merely a remnant of the former building,

but it has some very curious stones and memorials in it. One to John Elrington is a slab of sandstone with letters of pot-lead set into it. The font is a re-used Roman altar stone. If you have time it is worth going to see this church, one of the few structures remaining of the ancient village of Haydon.

At the junction with A69 cross the stile at field gate (R). This is a hay field so walk in single file towards gate at other side. The same applies in the next field, which is often under cultivation. At side of third field cross stile into Elrington Wood.

Beech, sycamore and oak here again, with ash and wych elm, and the ground covered with ramsons giving off their strong garlic smell. There is also cuckoo pint, or lords and ladies, or wild arum — whichever you like to call it — or even Arum maculatum to be absolutely correct.

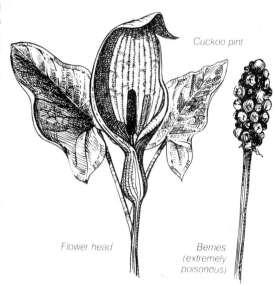

Cuckoo pint

Flower head

Berries (extremely poisonous)

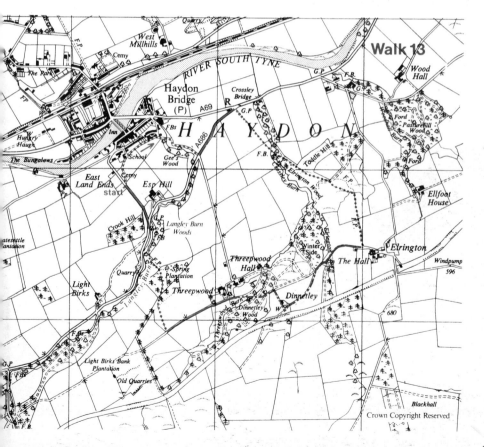

Walk 13

Crown Copyright Reserved

77

Footbridge crosses the Crossley Burn and path continues uphill with wall on left. At end of wall there are a number of paths so look for the waymarking and go straight on up to stile beside gate and blackthorn bushes.

The plantations now are mostly coniferous, much younger than the mature deciduous trees at the beginning of the wood, and the path is along what is called a 'ride' in forestry terms. It originated from Europe where people used these routes through the trees for riding along before mechanised transport was available. Forests and woods are divided into compartments for planting so the 'rides' mark the boundaries and are used as extraction routes after felling and also make useful fire breaks.

Cross stile into field and follow path keeping dry stone wall on the right, and then high dyke on left going towards Elrington.

Held of the Kings of Scotland for one knight's fee by a family called de Veteripont in the 13th century, Elrington was a considerable village; one of the 12 towns of Tynedale it included both the Hall Farm where you are now, and East Elrington on the left beyond the line of the railway. The estate was sold for £650 in 1627 to Sir Edward Radcliffe, father of the 1st Earl of Derwentwater, and thus after the 1715 Jacobite Rebellion suffered the fate of all the other Derwentwater properties: it was confiscated by the Crown and granted to the Governors of Greenwich Hospital. The Greenwich Commissioners sold the estate in the mid 1800s and despite its size in the Middle Ages, it is now only two farms with their cottages. The barn was at one time the Hall here.

The railway is the remains of the Hexham to Allendale railway opened in 1868 for freight and in 1869 for passengers. Of the two, freight was the more important as it carried the lead smelting products from Langley. In 1930 passenger traffic ceased altogether; the line was permanently closed and the track lifted in November 1950.

At Elrington turn right onto farm track and continue along top of pasture with old field boundary on your left. Pass through the gate at the stone bridge across the Elrington Burn.

This is an old bridge; notice the stepped stones downstream making a series of miniature waterfalls.

After bridge gate don't go through next gate but take left fork to Dinnetley. This is a very good farm track; without it,

View north near Elrington

Threepwood Hall

Dinnetley would be accessible only on foot or horseback.

Some places seem almost to exude an air of antiquity: Dinnetley is one of these. It, like Elrington, was confiscated with the other Derwentwater lands. The old railway line comes close and the arch ruins are clearly visible.

The waymarked path follows the garden wall (R), and then descends to Dinnetley Wood via a waymarked wicket. Turn left and follow path to plank bridge over Threepwood Burn.

This again is an oak, beech and sycamore wood, suggesting that the original wood started off with oaks, had beech specially planted, and was then invaded by sycamore. Here, in spring, bluebells carpet the woods in a haze of blue.

Continue uphill and leave wood at road, where Threepwood Hall appears in view.

The history of Threepwood goes back to Edwards III's time in the 13th century when it was a freehold in the Barony of Langley. Since then it has been owned by Lambtons, Stokoes, Featherstonehaughs and Aynsleys — all important Northumbrian families. The present house is Georgian in style. In 1825 George Lee, proprietor of the local lead mines, lived here. The name 'Threepwood' apparently meant 'debateable land'; that is, more than one claimant contended for title to it.

Turn left and walk along road.

On the right are views over the South Tyne and of the Whin Sill which, carrying Hadrian's Wall, is an ever present reminder that this area was once the frontier of the Roman Empire. And the cry of the curlew is a reminder that there is moorland immediately to the south, just as bleak as moors north of the Wall.

Continue until walls each side recess for gates. Just before signpost (R) turn right and squeeze through stone stile.

This type of stile is more typical of the Yorkshire Dales where it is known as the 'fat man's agony' (you can see why). Up here it is called a 'gap stile'.

Looking north from the stile you get a marvellous view of the farming pattern of part of the South Tyne valley; enclosed fields or arable and grazing with plenty of woodland in between for shelter, game preserves and investment.

Cross field to wind-blown larches, then following waymark go diagonally downhill to the kissing wicket and enter the Spring Plantation: mainly conifers with a thick carpet of pine needles. Leave plantation by stile. Walk down field to the stile in wall leading into Langley Burn Woods. Pass through woods, cross footbridge, turn right on A686, then left to Haydon Bridge cemetery.

A few hundred yards up the A686 (left) is the only memorial locally to James, Earl of Derwentwater, who was beheaded after the first Jacobite Rebellion. A grandson of Charles II, he was largely educated with his kinsman James (the Old Pretender), son of James II, and out of loyalty to him (but largely against his inclination) he joined the Jacobite forces in their ill-fated rebellion in 1715. He was taken after the Battle of Preston and beheaded the following year. A quiet family man, lavish of hospitality and much loved by his tenantry, he was greatly mourned and became almost a martyr in the North among the country folk.

The cross is a memorial to one of the biggest landowners in the County, and also to his brother Charles, beheaded after the 1745 rebellion. It was put up by Cadwallader Bates, a keen antiquarian, who bought and restored Langley Castle. It's not much to look at, it says very little, but it means a lot.

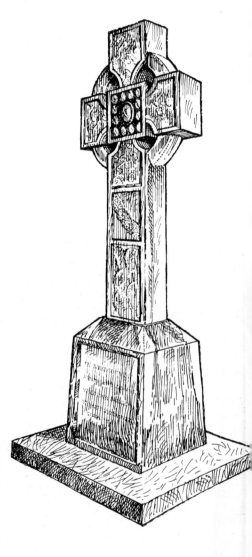

Derwentwater Memorial cross

Looking west along the River South Tyne at Haydon Bridge in the 1890's

Glossary

Bastle

A small fortified farmhouse with living accommodation for humans on the first floor and for livestock below. Term introduced in 15th century and common only in the border regions.

Border warfare

A state of unrest, at times of actual warfare, between England and Scotland from about 1300 to 1600. This lead to general unruliness among the inhabitants of the Borders who seemed to have more regard for their clan loyalties than for the law governing the rest of the country.

Drove road

Ancient unmetalled track for driving herds or flocks along.

Dyke or dike

A wall. People are sometimes confused by this because elsewhere in the country it means a ditch.

Haughland

Rich grassland by a river caused by deposits of sand and earth after floods or by the changes of water course. Pronounced 'halfland'.

Hemmel

Small stone single-storied building for cattle; usage now extends to include large, modern asbestos buildings, more like barns.

Leat

Open watercourse conducting water.

Lonnen

Lane.

March

Borderland. During the border warfares England and Scotland divided their border lands into east, middle and west marches as administrative areas, each under the control of a Lord Warden, the Sovereign's representative. A code of law drawn up and agreed by both the Scots and English in 1249 formed the basis of the laws over the next 300 years, and the Lord Wardens did their best to maintain them as they best understood them.

A typical bastle

Glossary

Military Road

Road between Newcastle and Carlisle started in 1751 on the suggestion of General Wade who 6 years earlier had been unable to transport his army from Newcastle to Carlisle during the 1745 Jacobite Rebellion.

Moss Trooper

Freebooter, thief (mostly of cattle); bands of them infested the mosses of the borderland, beyond the reach of the law.

Mule sheep

Hybrid sheep, usually a cross, in this region, between a Black-face ewe and a Border Leicester tup (ram).

Pele or peel

Originally a fortified enclosure; by 16th century a small square tower built in border counties of England and Scotland as a defence against forays. Often confused with or synonymous with 'bastle'.

Shielding

Custom of moving livestock to another region on a seasonal basis.

Shieling

Place on upland pasture (originally a small hut) used in summer only by persons practising shielding. Later used for any isolated cottage.

Sheep creep or smout

A small hole built into walls to allow sheep (or rabbits or water but in these cases the hole is smaller) to pass from one side of the wall to the other for pasture.

Sike or syke

Ditch or small burn.

Stell

An enclosure, usually a ring wall, for sheltering sheep; sometimes it is cross-shaped.

Township

The people living in a manor or parish, or the land area of it.

A stell

For further reading

*A GUIDE TO WALKING HADRIAN'S WALL
by G. Mizon
Hendon Publishing, 1977

* A WALK ALONG THE WALL
by Hunter Davies
Quartet Books, 1976

* HADRIAN'S WALL
by A. R. Birley
H.M.S.O., 1963

* HADRIAN'S WALL
by D. J. Breeze and B. Dobson
Penguin Books, 1978

HANDBOOK TO.THE ROMAN WALL
by J. Collingwood Bruce, ed. Charles Daniels
Harold Hill, 1978

* NORTHUMBERLAND — NATIONAL PARK GUIDE NO. 7
Edited by J. Philipson
H.M.S.O., 1969

* NORTHUMBRIAN CASTLES — TYNE AND ALLEN
by Frank Graham
Frank Graham, 1971

* SHORT GUIDE TO THE ROMAN WALL
by T. H. Rowland
Frank Graham, 1980

THE ARMY OF HADRIAN'S WALL
by B. Dobson and D. J. Breeze
Frank Graham, 1972

*HADRIAN'S WALL IN THE DAYS OF THE ROMANS
by Frank Graham
Frank Graham, 1984

*VINDOLANDA
by R. Birley
Thames and Hudson, 1977

* MAP OF HADRIAN'S WALL
Ordnance Survey, 1975

Titles marked * are available from the National Park Information Centre, Once Brewed